What IS Behind the Curtain?

Living the Resurrected Life

DEBORAH NEIBERGER - EXPRESSIONS OF HEARTLAND

ISBN-10:0991014618

ISBN-13: ISBN: 978-0-9910146-1-3

DEDICATION

I dedicate this book to my husband Michael whose strong faith and relentless love for Jesus has inspired many people. He displays the attributes of what it means to be strong and courageous for the Lord through many difficult trails. The 2012-2013 years have been a journey of trust and growth in relationship with Jesus Christ and Michael has taught me how to persevere through even the most complex situations. He brings hope to lives of many people and is an example of not just speaking the Word of God but living for him daily. I dedicate this book to him and am thankful for his encouragement and hard work to help me obey God in this project. I love you Sweetheart and marvel at God's wisdom in bringing us together in holy matrimony.

FOREWORD

At the core of every heart are undeniable cravings which must be satisfied. These cravings are quite demanding and steer our thoughts, motives and actions.

Inescapable cravings and longings. They drive us. They are inside of us. They must be gratified.

We crave true love. We were made for faithful love. We do strange things, thinking we are *getting* love, desperate to satisfy this craving.

In the absence of being liked or loved, all kinds of pain and anger can rise to the surface. Sometimes the ache is so intense we will frantically do something – anything – to cover up the pain. We resort to unhealthy and destructive ways to mend our need to be pursued and enjoyed.

Even if we try to deny our desire, it won't be dismissed. Symptoms of empty, pained hearts manifest all around us: raging outbursts, vodka hangovers, depression, suicide, broken marriages, entertainment addictions, distrust.

No matter what, we tend to seek assurance from people and circumstances that tell us we are enjoyed and loved. It's a natural response and is part of how we receive affirmation and fulfillment. But we are all broken people who are easily disappointed.

We need something or someone perfectly fitted for our heart longings and always faithful to tend to the depths of our soul.

"The source of my life comes from You," said David, a kingly man who desperately needed reassurance from God's faithful and loving heart (Ps 87:7). In Psalm 107:9 we read about God fulfilling our heart, our soul: "…He satisfies the longing soul, and fills the hungry soul with goodness" (Ps 107:9).

We were created by a God who enjoys loving us, and He designed us to need this assurance from Him. We are hard-wired to find complete satisfaction from God. Or, we could say it's in our DNA to be fulfilled by God.

Our journey to discover this kind of God who truly does and will complete us is the topic of Debi's book, ***What Is Behind the Curtain.*** She leads us into the unusual face-to-face posture before God and calls us to sit a while and listen to Him.

Debi's lifestyle declares, "Behold the Lamb." She helps point the way to receiving true peace in daily decisions and relationships. The apostle Paul pointed us to his primary life focus: to know Jesus as the Lamb. He wrote in 1 Corinthians 2:2, "For am I determined not to know anything among you except Jesus Christ and Him crucified [the Lamb that was slain]." And Jesus invited His friends to lean upon Him as the Servant Lamb: "Take My yoke upon you and learn from Me, for I am gentle and lowly in heart, and you will find rest for your souls" (Mt. 11:29).

For nearly 20 years I've watched Debi gaze upon God as her Source during the valley lows and mountain peak experiences. She loves God. Her testimony in thought, word and deed tells me that the God *first* choice changes everything.

Debi and I have joined together in prayer for people, cities and nations to know God's true nature and love. She partnered with my husband and me as we led corporate prayer for Orlando and Florida for several years. Debi's steadiness in faith influenced the establishing of houses of prayer in central Florida. There is much fruit to her credit deposited in her heavenly account.

What Is Behind the Curtain draws you into finding satisfaction from the one Person who intimately understands your make-up and carries your heart's blueprint. Each chapter invites you into beholding the Lamb in everyday life. I recommend **What Is Behind the Curtain** for anyone who desires to satisfy their love craving.

Sharon Gonzales
Founder and President of Joseph International, livelikejoseph.com
Author, Justice Wrapped in Mercy
Intercessory Missionary and Speaker

INTRODUCTION

I wrote this book because I began to think about the name of our church "New Covenant" and wonder why God chose this name for us at this time in history. I believe names are very significant part of God's destiny of our lives. As I began to pray over and study God's New Covenant a new appreciation and insight for this name began to rise up within me. God named places, people and even changed people's names throughout the Bible giving the meaning and purpose for their names. I believe that when we call someone by name we are reinforcing the character qualities given to the person and that names have significant impact in forming our identity. This is why many schools, businesses, churches and parents carefully chose names and even have Committees deliberate over the choice.

God's new covenant is his plan for our salvation and God freely gives it to us through his word. When we come to him, he begins a change in our lives that will continue forever because his shed blood is crying out for forgiveness rather than vengeance (Heb.12:24; Gen. 4:8-10). God has a magnificent plan for man and I am developing a greater desire for intimacy with the One who initiated it. His relentless love for us is beyond our comprehension.

Although I believe "What is Behind the Curtain" is a more appropriate name for this book, I am grateful for the inspiration from New Covenant Church.

This book's purpose is to exhort the people of God into a deeper relationship with God and can be studied as part of a small group or alone.

WHAT IS BEHIND THE CURTAIN?
LIVING THE RESURRECTED LIFE

"Having therefore, brethren, boldness to enter into the holiest by the blood of Jesus, By a new and living way, which he hath consecrated for us, through the veil (curtain), that is to say, his flesh; And having an high priest over the house of God; Let us draw near with a true heart in full assurance of faith, having our hearts sprinkled from an evil conscience, and our bodies washed with pure water. Let us hold fast the profession of our faith without wavering; (for he is faithful that promised ;) And let us consider one another to provoke unto love and to good works: Not forsaking the assembling of ourselves together, as the manner of some is; but exhorting one another: and so much the more, as ye see the day approaching." Hebrews 10:19-25

"Therefore if any man be in Christ, he is a new creature: old things are passed away; behold, all things are become new." 2 Corinthians 5:17

"For so an entrance shall be ministered unto you abundantly into the everlasting kingdom of our Lord and Saviour Jesus Christ." 2 Peter 1:11

"Fear not, little flock; for it is your Father's good pleasure to give you the kingdom." Luke 12:32

"But we have this treasure in earthen vessels, that the excellency of the power may be of God, and not of us." 2 Corinthians 4:7

"We were therefore buried with him through baptism into death in order that, just as Christ was raised from the dead through the glory of the Father, we too may live a new life. For if we have been united with him in a death like his, we will certainly also be united with him in a resurrection like his." Romans 6:4-5

TABLE OF CONTENTS

DEBORAH NEIBERGER

x

CHAPTER 1

RELENTLESS PURSUIT

I am grateful for the sovereignty of God in my life and his continual, relentless pursuit of me. Though I grew up in a Roman Catholic Church, I did not respond to the Lord's call until I was 23 years old in bondage to alcohol and drugs. It was a Tuesday night in 1980 when some friends asked me to meet them at Calvary Assembly of God's Rock House in Winter Park, Florida but they never came. I stayed and returned the following week, when the love of God overwhelmed me and I went forward to receive counsel. I told the people in the prayer room about my addiction and they asked me if I would like to give my life to the Lord, receive the baptism of the Holy Spirit, and pray I would get sick if I were to revert to addiction. I consented to all of this and the change it made in my life was astounding. My co-workers noticed a complete change in me and made comments about it because I was beaming with life and experiencing a depth of love that I never knew could exist. There was a hunger inside of me to know the Creator of the universe in ever-increasing ways. Instead of centering my attention on activities pertaining to the use of drugs and alcohol, I began meeting people at East India Ice Cream Parlor, or on Park Avenue, at prayer meetings, gathering at our apartment or the Rock House. There was joy, excitement and the assurance that the Lord is the One who sustains me through joys and trials of life, particularly the years of trauma and uncertainty.

It was during these excruciating circumstances that God used members of his body much like white blood cells to stop the bleeding and begin the healing process. We do not see the white blood cells in our body when we glance in the mirror but without these blood components, a paper cut would kill us. This concurs with the scripture that every member of the body is of critical importance. In other words, if you were not part of the body of Christ there would be a great deficiency. We are all integral parts of the body of Christ and it is imperative we understand this concept.

"Behold, the Lord that proclaimed unto the end of the world, Say ye to the daughter of Zion, Behold, thy salvation cometh; behold, his reward is with him, and his work before him. And they shall call them, The holy people, the redeemed of the Lord: and thou shalt be called Sought out, A city not forsaken." Isaiah 62:11-12

My husband Michael and I were reading Isaiah 62 and read the scripture about the Lord returning and bringing his reward with him. I looked at Michael and said, "We are the Lord's reward, the holy people and the people redeemed by the Lord". Can you look in the mirror and say, "I am the Lord's reward?" It is simply amazing that when we invite Jesus to be our Lord His presence is with us yet we may have a difficult time considering ourselves his reward. I remember how much I changed after Jesus Christ came into my life and that it felt like I was like crossing a curtain that separates the heavenly and earthly realms.

Journaling or Group Discussion Questions

1. Meditate on Isaiah 62:11-12 asking God for insight then, journal and/or discuss it in a small group or Bible study.

2. What feelings/thoughts come up inside you when you think about the Lord proclaiming his salvation and claiming you as his reward?

3. Write about a time you felt overwhelmed by his great love for you.

CHAPTER 2

WHAT IS BEHIND THE CURTAIN?

I searched through many boxes looking for meaning and answers to life. I plowed through doors and entered places I wish I had never gone yet none of them led me into the presence of God. It was only after Jesus Christ came into my life and His precious Holy Spirit filled my heart that everything changed. I entered a completely new world and as I stated earlier it was like crossing a curtain that separates the heaven from earthly realms. Thankfully, God does not force us to keep the big box or what we find behind the door but continually allows us the dignity to choose what is behind the (veil) curtain as stated in the New Living Translation.

"Having therefore, brethren, boldness to enter into the holiest by the blood of Jesus, By a new and living way, which he hath consecrated for us, through the veil (curtain), that is to say, his flesh; And having an high priest over the house of God; Let us draw near with a true heart in full assurance of faith, having our hearts sprinkled from an evil conscience, and our bodies washed with pure water. Let us hold fast the profession of our faith without wavering; (for he is faithful that promised;) And let us consider one another to provoke unto love and to good works: Not forsaking the assembling of ourselves together, as the manner of some is; but exhorting one another: and so much the more, as ye see the day approaching." Hebrews 10:19-25

A Spotless Lamb Production

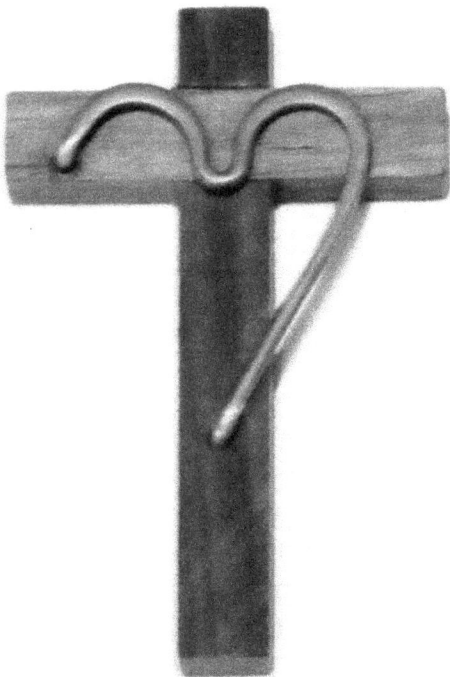

Made possible by the precious blood of Jesus

Deborah Neiberger © 2011
http://expressionsofheartland.wordpress.com/

Jesus himself is both our hope and the curtain that was torn open from top to bottom allowing us confident access into the very throne room of God.

"Wherefore the rather, brethren, give diligence to make your calling and election sure; for if ye do these things, ye shall never fall: For so an entrance shall be ministered unto you abundantly into the everlasting kingdom of our Lord and Saviour Jesus Christ." 2 Peter 1:10-11

Remember when Jesus breathed his last breath with "it is finished"; the curtain of the temple entrance into the Holy of Holies tore from top to bottom signifying that God himself split the curtain. He split it to provide open invitation for man to cross the threshold into that Holy Place by the blood of Jesus Christ, the sinless, spotless Lamb of God. God himself provided this lamb as the perfect sacrifice for our sins and the sins of the world.

One day I was driving my daughter to University of Florida returning from a holiday and a new song bubbled up inside of my heart expressing God's covenant love for us as our Redeemer.

Love Like No Other

Verse 1
Sacrifice Lamb, Jesus my Savior
Precious Redeemer and friend
You love me with a love that is like no other
A love I cannot comprehend, a love I cannot comprehend

(Chorus)
And I am overwhelmed by your love, overwhelmed by your love.
It's a love I cannot comprehend.

Verse 2
Sacrifice Lamb, You died for the nations
Suffered the sins of the world
Hell and the grave could not contain you
In victory you rose from the dead, in victory you rose from the dead

Verse 3
Jesus my Lord, Precious Redeemer
You poured out your life's blood for me
With your very life, you bought my salvation
Your love's my victory, Your love's my victory

As we walk behind the curtain, we begin to experience new victorious relationship with Jesus, the sacrifice Lamb and can enter into heaven itself. In Revelation 4 John gives us a glimpse of heaven...

The first thing he saw was a glorious throne with something as brilliant as sparkling diamonds, jasper and carnelian exuding from it. A radiant emerald tinted rainbow encircled it while bolts of lightning and peals of thunder emanated from it. Twenty-four other thrones surrounded this spectacular throne with twenty-four elders sitting on them wearing white robes and golden crowns. In front of this magnificent throne was a sea so peaceful that it appeared to be made of crystal, a golden bowl filled with incense, seven lamp stands with seven torches and four, six-winged creatures that were covered with eyes all around. Each being had different features; one looked like a lion, one like an ox, one like a man and one like an eagle. They could not contain themselves but continually cried, "Holy! Holy! Holy!" while the twenty-four elders fell to the ground and cast their crowns at the feet of the One who sat on the dazzling throne. These elders sang a new song, "Worthy is the Lamb..." the voices of a myriad of angels, and then every created thing in heaven, on earth and in the sea joined in a glorious crescendo of praise.

What a magnificent scene depicting the entranceway to the throne room of God Almighty and we are welcomed in because he has extended his scepter to each one of us and his invitation to, "Come up here." This throne room is in our hearts when we invite Jesus to come in and rule over our lives, we gain access through the curtain because of the blood of Jesus Christ. The kingdom of God is within us.

"Fear not, little flock; for it is your Father's good pleasure to give you the kingdom." Luke 12:32

"And when he was demanded of the Pharisees, when the kingdom of God should come, he answered them and said, the kingdom of God cometh not with observation: Neither shall they say, Lo here! Or, lo there! For behold the kingdom of God is within you…" Luke 17:20-21

Is it possible we can praise the Lord and permit him to reign in our daily lives? Yes, I believe that as we spend time prayer reading God's Word and listening quietly to Him, we allow him greater access into our lives because we are embracing the One who is the way, the truth and the life. It is through this time of loving submission that we can go forth in victory to love and serve the Lord with all of our heart, all of our soul, all of our mind and all of our strength and love our neighbors as ourselves. This is possible through his power alone and not through any innate ability that we possess. The great cloud of witness obtained a marvelous testimony by standing on the grace of God and keeping their eyes on Jesus, the champion who initiates and perfects our faith. (See Hebrews 12:2 NLT)

Walking in obedience to God shows our love for him and is the highest form of praise that we could possibly offer him.

"Praise ye the LORD. Praise the LORD, O my soul. While I live will I praise the LORD: I will sing praises unto my God while I have any being." Psalm 146:1-2

The entire Bible, not just the book of Psalms speaks about praising the Lord. It is critical to our lives as Christians. Praising God is not just singing songs to the Lord but we praise Him with our entire lives, in both the easy and the difficult times. In Exodus 15, the Israelites praised the Lord after he gave them a mighty victory against the Egyptians. Hezekiah praised the Lord asking him for direction as he spread out the letters from Sennacherib in 2 Kings 19. Shadrach, Meshach, and Abed-Nego went into the fiery furnace praising the Lord amidst the flames; Paul and the other Apostles praised the Lord while being held in prison and there are any more examples throughout the Word of God.

"He that hath my commandments, and keepeth them, he it is that loveth me: and he that loveth me shall be loved of my Father, and I will love him, and will manifest myself to him." John 14:21

What an awesome treasure that the God the universe would manifest or reveal himself to us! This treasure is available to us when we walk through the curtain open to us into the new life provided. We move from one world into another and our citizenship is now in heaven at the very throne of God himself, we have entered the Holy of Holies by the blood of Jesus.

It is possible to begin walking in the Kingdom of God in our daily lives as we build relationship with him and other believers. God knows everything about us and his Spirit will empower us to walk in his ways. We can ask him for this power daily because it is his grace alone that enables us able to walk in obedience to him.

Journaling or Group Discussion Questions

1. Meditate on Hebrews 10:19-25 asking God for insight then, journal and/or discuss it in a small group or Bible study.

2. What feelings/thoughts come up inside you when you think about what is behind the curtain?

3. Write about the time you became aware of Jesus Christ's invitation for you to enter into his presence. If you have not come to that realization yet, ask God for a revelation of his invitation to you.

CHAPTER 3

CROSSING THE THRESHOLD

Crossing the threshold behind the curtain encompasses much more than things we read depicting God's heavenly kingdom. What occurrence enabled us to gain access into this holy place?

"In the beginning God created the heaven and the earth." Genesis1:1

"And God said, Let us make man in our image, after our likeness: and let them have dominion over the fish of the sea, and over the fowl of the air, and over the cattle, and over all the earth, and over every creeping thing that creepeth upon the earth." Genesis 1:26

"...What is man, that thou art mindful of him? or the son of man that thou visitest him? Thou madest him a little lower than the angels; thou crownedst him with glory and honour, and didst set him over the works of thy hands: Thou hast put all things in subjection under his feet. For in that he put all in subjection under him, he left nothing that is not put under him. But now we see not yet all things put under him. But we see Jesus, who was made a little lower than the angels for the suffering of death, crowned with glory and honour; that he by the grace of God should taste death for every man. For it became him, for whom are all things, and by whom are all things, in bringing many sons unto glory, to make the captain of their salvation perfect through sufferings." Hebrews 2:6-10

"In the beginning God created the heavens and the earth," He spoke his "Let there be" and created man through his spoken word. God existed prior to the beginning of the created universe and according to Job "The Word of God, the breath of the Almighty is the giver of life."

The Word of God became human and dwelt among us but the very world he created did not recognize him. He was full of unfailing love and faithfulness and we have seen his glory, the glory of the Father's One and only Son. God revealed the law through Moses but his unfailing love and faithfulness came through Jesus Christ. Jesus is the one who reveals God to us, the one whom John the Baptist testified about who baptizes with the Holy Spirit. Jesus is the way, the truth and the life and no one comes to the Father except through him.

Jesus is the Lamb of God, the perfect sacrifice who suffered, died, was buried and rose again on the third day. He ascended unto the Father who promised to send us another advocate, the Holy Spirit to live in us and with us. He said that we would know that he is in the Father, we are in him and he is in us. How profound, we are one with God himself as the bride of Christ? "The Spirit and the bride say, Come", no wonder there is a cry in our hearts to abide in his word and let him abide in us.

"Let the word of Christ dwell in you richly in all wisdom; teaching and admonishing one another in psalms and hymns and spiritual songs, singing with grace in your hearts to the Lord." Colossians 3:16

"If ye abide in me, and my words abide in you, ye shall ask what ye will, and it shall be done unto you. Herein is my Father glorified, that ye bear much fruit; so shall ye be my disciples." John 15:7-8

"It is the spirit that quickeneth; the flesh profiteth nothing: the words that I speak unto you, they are spirit, and they are life." John 6:63

"For the word of God is quick, and powerful, and sharper than any two edged sword, piercing even to the dividing asunder of soul and spirit, and of the joints and marrow, and is a discerner of the thoughts and intents of the heart." Hebrews 4:12

God's Word is the very breath of life performing his will from inside of us through his precious Holy Spirit and is the same Word that was with God in the beginning. Whether we speak, sing, or read his word, the very life of Jesus Christ is proceeding from our mouths influencing the things around us because his words are life and peace. His word moves molecules, destroys sickness, brings life to that which is dead and moves on the hearts of men. He watches over his word to perform it because honors his word and says signs should follow them that believe in the name of Jesus. His word is sharper than a two-edged sword and cutting through soul and spirit as we speak. This word illustrates to us what is of him and what is of the flesh, what is good, what is evil exposing our innermost thoughts and desires.

Even though Jesus is in heaven, he is here in the midst of us because his Holy Spirit dwells inside of us. It is beyond our comprehension to grasp the concept of our eternal God.

Years ago, I listened to a wise Catholic priest teach about eternal life. He talked about how a baby carried in the womb, fed by the mother, held tightly and kept warm is being prepared to enter another world that he knows nothing about. Then, at the proper time, he is thrust out into a cold, unfamiliar world fully equipped to function. The man was preaching at a funeral and compared our lives today as preparation for the next phase of our existence for which we are empowered to choose life or death.

"I call heaven and earth to record this day against you, that I have set before you life and death, blessing and cursing: therefore choose life, that both thou and thy seed may live!" Deuteronomy 30:19

"Jesus saith unto him, I am the way, the truth, and the life: no man cometh unto the Father, but by me." John 14:6

"Whosoever believeth that Jesus is the Christ is born of God: and every one that loveth him that begat loveth him also that is begotten of him." 1 John 5:1

"And this is the record, that God hath given to us eternal life, and this life is in his Son. He that hath the Son hath life; and he that hath not the Son of God hath not life. These things have I written unto you that believe on the name of the Son of God; that ye may know that ye have eternal life, and that ye may believe on the name of the Son of God." 1 John 5:11-13

"But we speak the wisdom of God in a mystery, even the hidden wisdom, which God ordained before the world unto our glory: Which none of the princes of this world knew: for had they known it, they would not have crucified the Lord of glory. But as it is written, Eye hath not seen, nor ear heard, neither have entered into the heart of man, the things which God hath prepared for them that love him." 1 Corinthians 2:7-9

When we choose life (Jesus) we can begin to grow and develop much like the baby in the mother's womb and are being fully equipped to function in our daily lives, as well as the next phase of our existence. 2 Peter 1:5-11 talks about this growth and development. I encourage you to prayerfully read and apply these passages to your life. The last verse 2 Peter 1:11 from the New Living Translation really intrigued me as a promise that God blesses these choices because it says he gives us a grand entrance into his kingdom.

"And to her was granted that she should be arrayed in fine linen, clean and white: for the fine linen is the righteousness of saints. And he saith unto me, Write, Blessed are they which are called unto the marriage supper of the Lamb. And he saith unto me, These are the true sayings of God." Revelations 19:8-9

I began to consider what this could possibly entail and many ideas came to mind. One day Father Carl talked about a prestigious banquet where there is an announcement as each person makes their entrance, arrayed in beautiful garments and escorted to an extravagantly prepared banquet table. The table adorned with elegant décor and gifts specifically selected for the person assigned to that setting. The best part of the whole banquet is that we can dine with the King of Kings and Lord of Lords himself. This is probably a trivial expression of the marriage supper of the Lamb because it is beyond our wildest dreams.

The love of God passes knowledge but He will freely reveal His love to those who seek this treasure beyond comprehension.

"Of his own will begat he us with the word of truth, that we should be a kind of firstfruits of his creatures." James 1:18

God created us to fellowship with him because of his great love for us. Take some time to think about this great love that God loved us so much that he gave his only begotten Son that we might live with him forever because we are his prized possession!

Journaling or Group Discussion Questions

1. What scriptures in this chapter had the greatest impact on you?

2. Journal about what God is saying to you through these scriptures.

3. What is God saying to you specifically through James 1:18?

CHAPTER 4

MESSIAH, SUFFERING SERVANT

Let us take a deeper look at Jesus the Messiah the Lord's Suffering Servant, the King and Creator of the Universe.

"Behold, my servant shall deal prudently, he shall be exalted and extolled, and be very high. As many were astonished at thee; his visage was so marred more than any man, and his form more than the sons of men: So shall he sprinkle many nations; the kings shall shut their mouths at him: for that which had not been told them shall they see; and that which they had not heard shall they consider. Who hath believed our report? and to whom is the arm of the LORD revealed? For he shall grow up before him as a tender plant, and as a root out of a dry ground: he hath no form nor comeliness; and when we shall see him, there is no beauty that we should desire him. He is despised and rejected of men; a man of sorrows, and acquainted with grief: and we hid as it were our faces from him; he was despised, and we esteemed him not. Surely he hath borne our griefs, and carried our sorrows: yet we did esteem him stricken, smitten of God, and afflicted. But he was wounded for our transgressions, he was bruised for our iniquities: the chastisement of our peace was upon him; and with his stripes we are healed. All we like sheep have gone astray; we have turned every one to his own way; and the LORD hath laid on him the iniquity of us all. He was oppressed, and he was afflicted, yet he opened not his mouth: he is brought as a lamb to the slaughter, and as a sheep before her shearers is dumb, so he openeth not his mouth. He was taken from prison and from judgment: and who shall declare his generation? for he was cut off out of the land of the living: for the transgression of my people was he stricken. And he made his grave with the wicked, and with the rich in his death; because he had done no violence, neither was any deceit in his mouth. Yet it pleased the LORD to bruise him; he hath put him to grief: when thou shalt make his soul an offering for sin, he shall see his seed, he shall prolong his days, and the pleasure of the LORD shall prosper in his hand. He shall see of the travail of his soul, and shall be satisfied: by his knowledge shall my righteous servant justify many; for he shall bear their iniquities. Therefore will I divide him a portion with the great, and he shall divide the spoil with the strong; because he hath poured out his soul unto death: and he was numbered with the transgressors; and he bare the sin of many, and made intercession for the transgressors." Isaiah 52:13-53:12

Isaiah prophetically wrote that the Messiah will prosper but it did not necessarily appear that way when we look at the circumstances surrounding his life and death.

People expected the Messiah to come and reign on earth as the King that he is but he had a humble and surprising earthly existence right from the beginning. His life story written throughout the Bible is an amazing narrative of which he honors us to be partakers. The words of Father Christopher left great impact on my heart as he spoke about being partakers and not spectators of Jesus' glorious life. In the book of Hebrews, the great cloud of witnesses is cheering us on and by faith; God gave them a vision and prayer for our lives in the distance. Hebrews 11:39 affirms that these people are not complete without seeing the promises of God fulfilled through us and we are not complete without them.

"And these all, having obtained a good report through faith, received not the promise: God having

provided some better thing for us, that they without us should not be made perfect." Hebrews 11:39-40

Driving home from work one day the above scripture bubbled up inside of me. I kept thinking about the promises to many of the saints, like Abraham who has more children than the stars in the sky, John the Baptist crying in the wilderness to prepare the way of the Lord, the Apostles preaching the Gospel. Likewise, aunts, uncles, grandparents or parents who cried out to God for our salvation and passed on are also among this great cloud of witnesses. We are part of the promise God gave them, they watch from a distance, cheering us on and the Bible says that they would not be complete without us. Reading this makes me realize that we would not be here without them because God looked ahead at the joy set before him and embraced the cross, disregarding its shame and is now seated in the place of honor at the right hand of the Father. (See Hebrews 12:1-3)

It is exciting that God uses people in our daily life to empower us to move forward with his vision. God is using many people in my life right now in profound ways. I cannot even begin to understand what he is doing. I only know that we cannot live without other people in our lives but must move forward together as a community of believers. I see God building church community in deep and profound ways because of the work he is getting ready to perform on this earth. Every part of the body is critical, from the smallest baby to the oldest adult. Sometimes we are weak and need the care of others and sometimes we are strong and need to give care to others. It keeps harmony among the members and we can give care to each other. We are truly interdependent and God uses that to enable each other to grow and be free.

I had the opportunity to experience his healing touch through the body of Christ, because I went through four church splits in various denominations. I knew that I was not the cause of the splits, but just being a church member I did contribute to things that happened, particularly being in leadership or on staff. I was getting tired of wandering around the desert and did not want to do it again. We were getting ready to become part of another church, I knew God wanted us there and was terrified. I began to ask God to show me attitudes, words and actions in me that could bring healing to this area of my life and in his faithfulness; He did show me several painful things.

He also showed me things that He was happy with and wanted me to continue to do. It was a very difficult time in my life, but well worth it. He gave me this vision regarding broken relationships in the body of Christ.

I saw the people of God who were broken and hurt in relationships in the body of Christ and they looked like sheets of colored glass. The sheets shattered and broke because of the sin and the strife that took place within His body. God swept the pieces of glass into a heap and began to put them back together as one, like a beautiful stained glass window. I watched in amazement. He worked and put each piece carefully together until there was no longer any division among us. His light began to shine through the glass and I saw a picture of Jesus, the Healer. He is the One that holds the pieces together to form this beautiful stained glass window. Jesus took the stain of our sin and formed it into this thing of beauty. The light of His love shines through every little piece of broken glass to make it sparkle like a diamond showing its own particular color to make this window into a glorious expression of Christ. He makes all things new.

Now back to the story of Jesus who makes all this possible in our lives. The story of his life begins further back than we can possibly imagine so let us begin with the obscure, unmarried, pregnant, teenage girl who was carrying the Savior of the world. Joseph her fiancé married her regardless of the circumstances surrounding her pregnancy because an angel spoke to him about Jesus being the child of promise despite probable disagreement of family and friends.

In the earthly realm this marriage and the birth of this child appears to begin on shaky ground. There were a few family members and shepherds that God gave a revelation of Jesus but the majority of the people were blind to it.

Jesus grew up in the presence of the Lord quietly living in the home of a carpenter and not the palace of some great king. He was acquainted with sorrow and grief showing his compassion to the people he encountered through healing and provision of their basic needs. He regarded the needs of these people over the law by laying hands on sick and dead people bringing life while he himself became unclean according to Jewish law. This infuriated the religious community but Jesus fulfilled the scriptures that say he himself carried our weaknesses, sicknesses and sorrow. Reviled because he ate with sinners and tax collectors Jesus continued to demonstrate the love of the Father. He was condemned unjustly because of the jealousy, pride and legalism of religious leaders but this was part of the Lord's plan. The rejection and harsh treatment were actually the will of the Father to prosper him. When Jesus saw all that he accomplished through his sufferings, he was satisfied because he bore our sins making it possible for us to become righteous. (Isaiah 53) It is for this reason God gave him the honors of a victorious soldier who now sits at the right hand of the Father while his enemies are a footstool for his feet. He interceded for us rebels and we now are welcome into the throne room of God along with him.

One Sunday during worship service, while we sang a song about trials and pain a particular scripture kept coming up inside of me.

"Looking unto Jesus the author and finisher of our faith; who for the joy that was set before him endured the cross, despising the shame, and is set down at the right hand of the throne of God." Hebrews 12:2

It was so intense that I actually found myself shouting out "who for the joy that was set before him endured the cross." This word was so vivid and passionate in my spirit that I actually felt the overwhelming love of God engulfing me. I saw Jesus hanging on the cross before an angry crowd jeering and mocking him yet he looked beyond the crowd to the joy set before him. What was he looking at in the crowd that brought him such great joy? It was the very people mocking and jeering him, he saw us as His precious bride and inspired by immense love he suffered crucifixion to bring us eternal life. What kind of love is this and how is it possible to live in this love?

"The love of God is shed abroad in our hearts by the Holy Ghost which is given unto us." Romans 5:5

We are the ones that sinned; Jesus dies for us and then leaves us with the gift of his precious Holy Spirit. Is there anything more awesome anything greater than this? I cannot think of one solitary thing that I would rather have in life than a love relationship with the very God of all creation.

I stopped to ponder the scripture from Luke 12:48....

"...For unto whomsoever much is given, of him shall be much required: and to who men have committed much, of him they will ask the more." Luke 12:48

How much more could God give than the life of His Son Jesus and the impartation of His precious Holy Spirit through whom we have power to become the children of God?

How do we respond to such a great love as this? We can ask precious Holy Spirit, the very flame of God to fill us with His love daily and empower us to hear his voice, feel his emotions, and give us his vision to see what he sees.

"And we desire that every one of you do shew the same diligence to the full assurance of hope unto the end: That ye be not slothful, but followers of them who through faith and patience inherit the promises. For when God made promise to Abraham, because he could swear by no greater, he sware by himself, Saying, Surely blessing I will bless thee, and multiplying I will multiply thee. And so, after he had patiently endured, he obtained the promise. For men verily swear by the greater: and an oath for confirmation is to them an end of all strife. Wherein God, willing more abundantly to shew unto the heirs of promise the immutability of his counsel, confirmed it by an oath: That by two immutable things, in which it was impossible for God to lie, we might have a strong consolation, who have fled for refuge to lay hold upon the hope set before us: Which hope we have as an anchor of the soul, both sure and stedfast, and which entereth into that within the veil; Whither the forerunner is for us entered, even Jesus, made an high priest for ever after the order of Melchisedec." Hebrews 6:11-20

This short passage in Hebrews is overflowing with profound examples of what it means to give your word or make a promise. A long time ago, prior to the need for legal contracts in which people look for excuses to alleviate the commitments they made; an individual's word had significance. When someone gave their word and shook hands, it was a binding pledge or vow; however, society has changed immensely. While it is true that society has changed, the Word of God never changes. The Word of God defines our lives as Christians, not the standards determined by society. God's Word is a covenant contract sealed with the blood of Jesus, which leads us to the inner sanctuary of God who hears not only our spoken words but the very cries of our hearts. Once again, God is commanding us to follow his example that giving our word is a binding oath and reminding us that his word is an undisputable fact, which will come to fruition. The first example of course is his love for us, which is unchanging and he promises we will inherit his kingdom. This example is an undeniable truth because God swore to us in an oath that he made in his own name and there is no greater name in heaven, on earth or under the earth. We can stand on the truth written in his word that without question his oath is binding, he will not change his mind because it is impossible for God to lie. Since, God made this oath, we have an anchor of hope to steady us and hold us firm as we face the challenging storms of this life. It is as we begin to trust in God's unchanging Word that we become strong entering into his inner sanctuary of rest.

Consider for a moment that each time you read, speak, sing, teach, preach, confess and/or proclaim God's Word you are not only reminding him of his commitment to us but are also making an oath to him. It is a covenant relationship because the blood of Jesus Christ himself seals it and this makes it obligatory; a legal contract sealed in heaven by his blood.

"He is the mediator of the new testament, that by means of death, for the redemption of the transgressions that were under the first testament, they which are called might receive the promise of

eternal inheritance. For where a testament is, there must also of necessity be the death of the testator. For a testament is of force after men are dead: otherwise it is of no strength at all while the testator liveth. Whereupon neither the first testament was dedicated without blood. For when Moses had spoken every precept to all the people according to the law, he took the blood of calves and of goats, with water, and scarlet wool, and hyssop, and sprinkled both the book, and all the people, Saying, This is the blood of the testament which God hath enjoined unto you. Moreover he sprinkled with blood both the tabernacle, and all the vessels of the ministry. And almost all things are by the law purged with blood; and without shedding of blood is no remission. It was therefore necessary that the patterns of things in the heavens should be purified with these; but the heavenly things themselves with better sacrifices than these. For Christ is not entered into the holy places made with hands, which are the figures of the true; but into heaven itself, now to appear in the presence of God for us: Nor yet that he should offer himself often, as the high priest entereth into the holy place every year with blood of others; For then must he often have suffered since the foundation of the world: but now once in the end of the world hath he appeared to put away sin by the sacrifice of himself." Hebrews 9:15-26

The New Living Translation calls the testament a will and that in order for a will to valid it is necessary to prove the death of the one who wrote it. Jesus Christ entered heaven itself to appear in the presence of God and present his blood as proof of his death. He offered his blood once for all time to set us free because without the shedding of blood there is no remission of sin. God's will is in place because Jesus Christ offered himself as the sacrifice lamb.

" For the law made nothing perfect, but the bringing in of a better hope did; by the which we draw nigh unto God. And inasmuch as not without an oath he was made priest: (For those priests were made without an oath; but this with an oath by him that said unto him, The Lord sware and will not repent, Thou art a priest for ever after the order of Melchisedec:) By so much was Jesus made a surety of a better testament." Hebrews 7:19-22

What are we doing when we pray, when we confess our faith through the Apostles Creed, Nicene Creed, sinner's prayer or covenants of baptism, communion and marriage? Is it mere ritual or does it carry weight in heaven, on earth and under the earth? Are there eyewitnesses involved here, like people, angels, demons, a great cloud of witnesses, and above all God himself? Who is listening when we speak to our spouses, children, friends, coworkers, neighbors or anyone else? What kind of impact do our unseen words, thoughts and even attitudes have on the world around us and do they really affect our destiny? Does God really hold us accountable?

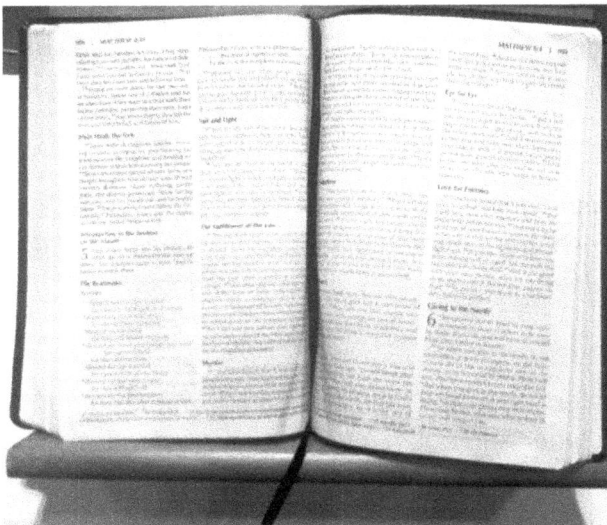

These are all rhetorical questions prompting us to consider the implications of the words we speak, how they do influence our daily lives and the surrounding environment. Read the words of the Apostles Creed aloud and contemplate the confession you are making with your mouth allowing it to penetrate your heart knowing that everyone around you; human, angel, demon, every created thing and God himself are witnessing our confession and bask in God's promises of eternal life.

> ### *The Apostle's Creed*
>
> *I believe in God, the Father Almighty,*
> *Creator of Heaven and Earth*
> *And in Jesus Christ*
> *His only Son, Our Lord*
> *Who was conceived of the Holy Spirit*
> *Born of the Virgin Mary*
> *Suffered under Pontius Pilate*
> *Was crucified, died and was buried.*
> *On the third day, he rose again*
> *He ascended into Heaven*
> *and is seated at the right hand*
> *of God, the Father Almighty.*
> *He will come again to judge the living and the dead.*
> *I believe in the Holy Spirit,*
> *the Holy Catholic Church,*
> *the Communion of Saints,*
> *the forgiveness of sins,*
> *the resurrection of the body,*
> *and life everlasting.*
> *Amen*

The Apostles Creed is a terrific confession of our faith and a demonstration of the reverence and unity the Godhead displays to the church. He also commands us to love each other the way He loves us (John 15:12) and the book of Hebrews exemplifies both the love and honor the Godhead displays.

Hebrews 1-3 is a profound example of the Blessed Trinity loving, honoring and preferring each other. I never realized the great display of affection and reverence given one to the other in this book of the Bible. In Hebrews 1:8-12, the Father is talking to the Son and says, *"Your throne, O God, is for ever and ever: a scepter of righteousness is the scepter of your kingdom. Thou has loved righteousness, and hated iniquity; therefore God, even thy God, hath anointed thee with the oil of gladness above thy fellows."*

He also says to the Son, *"And, Thou, Lord, in the beginning has laid the foundation of the earth; and the heavens are the works of thine hands: They shall perish; but hour remainest; and they all shall wax old as doth a garment; And as a vesture shalt thou fold them up, and they shall be changed: but thou art the same, and thy years shall not fail."*

Then, in Hebrews 2:12-13, the Son speaks to the Father saying, *"I will declare thy name unto my brethren, in the midst of the church will I sing praise unto thee. And again, I will put my trust in him. And again, Behold I and the children which God that given me."*

Reading on into Hebrews 3:7-8, the Holy Spirit is speaking: *"Wherefore (as the Holy Ghost saith, To day if ye will hear his voice, Harden not your hearts, as in the provocation, in the day of temptation in the wilderness"*

This is an example of the perfect unity that Jesus is referring to in John 17:22-23, *"And the glory which thou gavest me I have given them; that they may be one, even as we are one: I in them, and thou in me, that they may be made perfect in one; and that the world may know that thou hast sent me, and hast loved them, as thou hast loved me."*

We have been studying about God's love for his church but these scriptures show us his love for himself. This is important as he tells us to love our neighbors as ourselves and sets the example of this great love and reverence in the scriptures outlined above. If we do not love ourselves, we will not be able to love our neighbors and this is not selfishness but self-respect and self-worth.

Journaling or Group Discussion Questions

1. What are some of the ways you observe the reverence of God expressed in life and creation?

2. Journal or discuss ways that you can express the reverence of God in your daily life.

3. Journal or discuss a time when God freed you from a deep hurt or situation in your life.

CHAPTER 5

THIS IS MY BELOVED

"And so it is written, the first man Adam was made a living soul; the last Adam was made a quickening spirit. Howbeit that was not first which is spiritual, but that which is natural; and afterward that which is spiritual. The first man is of the earth, earthy; the second man is the Lord from heaven. As is the earthy, such are they also that are earthy: and as is the heavenly, such are they also that are heavenly. And as we have borne the image of the earthy, we shall also bear the image of the heavenly. Now this I say, brethren, that flesh and blood cannot inherit the kingdom of God; neither doth corruption inherit incorruption. Behold, I shew you a mystery; We shall not all sleep, but we shall all be changed, In a moment, in the twinkling of an eye, at the last trump: for the trumpet shall sound, and the dead shall be raised incorruptible, and we shall be changed. For this corruptible must put on incorruption, and this mortal must put on immortality. So when this corruptible shall have put on incorruption, and this mortal shall have put on immortality, then shall be brought to pass the saying that is written, Death is swallowed up in victory. O death, where is thy sting? O grave, where is thy victory? The sting of death is sin; and the strength of sin is the law. But thanks be to God, which giveth us the victory through our Lord Jesus Christ. Therefore, my beloved brethren, be ye stedfast, unmoveable, always abounding in the work of the Lord, forasmuch as ye know that your labour is not in vain in the Lord." 1 Corinthians 15:45-58

Jesus always brings us the victory. We stand on his promises because he paid our debit in full.

"But we have this treasure in earthen vessels, that the excellency of the power may be of God, and not of us." 2 Corinthians 4:7

Whenever you hear accusations coming up from inside of you remember the words that God thunders over you, "This is my beloved child in who I am delighted". Speak forth this truth, "Jesus shed his blood for me and placed his treasured Holy Spirit inside me," then, throw yourself on the mercy of the shed blood of Jesus and be reconciled to God.

We can understand more about the love of God and some of his great plan for us in John 9 when we read about the man born blind.

"Now as Jesus passed by, He saw a man who was blind from birth. And His disciples asked Him, saying, "Rabbi, who sinned, this man or his parents, that he was born blind?" Jesus answered, "Neither this man nor his parents sinned, but that the works of God should be revealed in him. I must work the works of Him who sent Me while it is day; the night is coming when no one can work. As long as I am in the world, I am the light of the world." When He had said these things, He spat on the ground and made clay with the saliva; and He anointed the eyes of the blind man with the clay. And He said to him, "Go, wash in the pool of Siloam" (which is translated, Sent). So he went and washed, and came back seeing." John 9:1-7

In John 9, Jesus and his disciples see a man who is blind from birth but it does not say that the man was aware of their presence or even knew who Jesus was. I found this story intriguing because Jesus and his disciples, apparently passing by this man noticed his blindness. The disciples questioned Jesus regarding the cause of this blindness but Jesus already had a plan to heal him and reveal God's glory. Jesus patiently answers their questions just as he does our questions but the dichotomy of God's point of view verses ours brought the scripture below to the forefront of my mind.

"For My thoughts are not your thoughts, Nor are your ways My ways," says the LORD. "For as the heavens are higher than the earth, So are My ways higher than your ways, And My thoughts than your thoughts." Isaiah 55:8-9

So many times, I find my thoughts focus on the natural realm and I miss the higher purposes of God. Jesus apparently does not mind our questioning; he understands our humanity and gladly reveals his higher purposes to us, when we inquire.

The disciples watch Jesus as he takes the dirt from the ground and mixes it with his own saliva, thus forming clay rubbing it in the man's eyes.

"For it is the God who commanded light to shine out of darkness, who has shone in our hearts to give the light of the knowledge of the glory of God in the face of Jesus Christ. But we have this treasure in earthen vessels, that the excellence of the power may be of God and not of us." 2 Corinthians 4:6-7

Some translations describe the earthen vessels as clay vessels and God's light shines through us clay vessels demonstrating his love for humanity. We witness the love and compassion of Jesus displayed through the healing of this blind man thus bringing glory to God, yet we observe the religious community so outraged by his actions that they cast the previously blind man out of the Synagogue. God in his great love preplanned this entire event to reveal Jesus Christ to this one man and then sent him to wash in the pool of Siloam (sent). I believe this pool is symbolic of the baptism of the Holy Spirit as preparation to share the Gospel with the least, the lost and the lonely. God uses us, simple earthen vessels to display his glory to a lost and dying world, thus allowing us to be participants and not simply observers of his great story.

"Jesus heard that they had cast him out; and when He had found him, He said to him, "Do you believe in the Son of God?" He answered and said, "Who is He, Lord, that I may believe in Him?" And Jesus said to him, "You have both seen Him and it is He who is talking with you." Then he said, "Lord, I believe!" And he worshiped Him. And Jesus said, "For judgment I have come into this world, that those who do not see may see, and that those who see may be made blind. Then some of the Pharisees who were with Him heard these words, and said to Him, "Are we blind also?" Jesus said to them, "If you were blind, you would have no sin; but now you say, 'We see.' Therefore your sin remains." John 9:35-41

Journaling or Group Discussion Questions

1. How do you see yourself as God's beloved child in whom he is well pleased?

2. Ask God what he would like to tell you about being his beloved child.

3. What is God saying to you through 2 Corinthians 4:6-7?

CHAPTER 6

WELCOME TO THE RESURRECTED LIFE

"The first day of the week cometh Mary Magdalene early, when it was yet dark, unto the sepulchre, and seeth the stone taken away from the sepulchre. Then she runneth, and cometh to Simon Peter, and to the other disciple, whom Jesus loved, and saith unto them, They have taken away the LORD out of the sepulchre, and we know not where they have laid him. Peter therefore went forth, and that other disciple, and came to the sepulchre. So they ran both together: and the other disciple did outrun Peter, and came first to the sepulchre. And he stooping down, and looking in, saw the linen clothes lying; yet went he not in. Then cometh Simon Peter following him, and went into the sepulchre, and seeth the linen clothes lie, And the napkin, that was about his head, not lying with the linen clothes, but wrapped together in a place by itself. Then went in also that other disciple, which came first to the sepulchre, and he saw, and believed. For as yet they knew not the scripture, that he must rise again from the dead. Then the disciples went away again unto their own home". John 20:1-10

After hearing Mary Magdalene's story, Peter and the other disciples began running toward the tomb. The very first thing they observed when looking inside was the strips of linen laying there and the burial cloth that was by itself folded away from the rest of the grave cloths. They still did not understand that Jesus had to rise from the dead.

I began to ask the Lord some questions, "First of all, why were the strips of linen just cast off to the side?" "Lord, why was the burial cloth that wrapped around your head laying aside by itself all neatly folded? It appeared that God removed the linen cloth in haste but neatly folded the burial cloth, setting it to the side. Why is this written this way and what makes the two different?"

I kept thinking of the stone rolled away as symbolic of my obstructed ability to understand the meaning of the death and resurrection of Christ, which was the first thing he removed so I could make a commitment to him. I know that the only one that could accomplish this was God himself. He sent his loving laborers to share with me and then at his chosen time he opened up my heart to understand the scriptures, enabling me to make an affirmation of faith in him. I pondered the linen cloths quickly cast off and how in my own life it symbolized the world and its ways. This apparently done in haste and reminded me of Romans 6:2-14, which speaks of our baptismal covenant.

"God forbid. How shall we, that are dead to sin, live any longer therein? Know ye not, that so many of us as were baptized into Jesus Christ were baptized into his death? Therefore we are buried with him by baptism into death: that like as Christ was raised up from the dead by the glory of the Father, even so we also should walk in newness of life. For if we have been planted together in the likeness of his death, we shall be also in the likeness of his resurrection: Knowing this, that our old man is crucified with him, that the body of sin might be destroyed, that henceforth we should not serve sin. For he that is dead is freed from sin. Now if we be dead with Christ, we believe that we shall also live with him: Knowing that Christ being raised from the dead dieth no more; death hath no more dominion over him. For in that he died, he died unto sin once: but in that he liveth, he liveth unto God. Likewise reckon ye also yourselves to be dead indeed unto sin, but alive unto God through Jesus Christ our Lord. Let not

sin therefore reign in your mortal body, that ye should obey it in the lusts thereof. Neither yield ye your members as instruments of unrighteousness unto sin: but yield yourselves unto God, as those that are alive from the dead, and your members as instruments of righteousness unto God. For sin shall not have dominion over you: for ye are not under the law, but under grace." Romans 6:2-14

"For God so loved the world, that he gave his only begotten Son, that whosoever believeth in him should not perish, but have everlasting life." John 3:16

This familiar passage is probably one of the first verses we learn in Sunday school but we may never have stopped to consider the intensity of this statement. It is so powerful; it speaks of our identification with the death and resurrection of our Lord Jesus Christ.

"I am crucified with Christ: nevertheless I live; yet not I, but Christ liveth in me: and the life which I now live in the flesh I live by the faith of the Son of God, who loved me, and gave himself for me." Galatians 2:20

When we obey him through baptism, we are making the above proclamation to every living creature on earth, in heaven and under the earth. It is our testimony, a binding oath that we are choosing to live our lives for Jesus Christ and have committed high treason against the kingdom of darkness and our own fleshly desire. We die to our old nature and enter into a new life in Christ Jesus; we are indeed new creatures. His Holy Spirit, the same Spirit that raised Jesus Christ from the dead is now resident in us and we are choosing transformation to the image of Jesus Christ.

"We were therefore buried with him through baptism into death in order that, just as Christ was raised from the dead through the glory of the Father, we too may live a new life. For if we have been united with him in a death like his, we will certainly also be united with him in a resurrection like his." Romans 6:4-5

"Therefore if any man be in Christ, he is a new creature: old things are passed away; behold, all things are become new." 2 Corinthians 5:17

Our baptism is a commitment to live the crucified life. It is a proclamation that speaks into all of heaven, earth and all creatures under the earth that we are choosing to embrace the cross of Jesus Christ. Our decision to make Jesus Christ Lord and Savior is a covenant he cut with us and the acceptance of a covenant sealed in the waters of baptism. This means that at baptism we not only forgiven of sin but the waters of baptism signify the burial of the old life and the resurrection to new life in Christ. He willfully chose to die for us (burial cloths cautiously removed and folded away from the linen), God carefully planned and lovingly executed our salvation by the sealed blood of Jesus through his death on the cross and victorious resurrection. The entire process accomplished exclusively by his grace and we could not achieve in our flesh, so on one hand the initial act of throwing off the old brings us into a new kingdom and we are new creations. The Holy Spirit moves in and takes up residence in our hearts. Adopted into the family of God, we cry out "Abba Father", completely accepted by God because Jesus Christ purchased our salvation. The Father was ecstatic with his Son's obedience and our renewed relationship with him, like Mary Magdalene we can say, "I have seen the Lord", running to tell others what he has done for us. On the other hand, just like any other child we need to grow and learn to live this crucified and resurrected life. I believe that is symbolic of the careful removal, folding and placing of burial cloth away from the linen strips. We must embrace the cross in our own lives daily because without death there is no resurrection. We must appear before God completely naked, allowing him to clothe us with his righteousness alone. We have absolutely nothing to offer him because God's grace alone that validates the transaction of his new covenant.

When we come to him daily, we are developing our relationship with him and allowing Him to transform our hearts into his glorious image. Romans 12:2 discusses the renewal of our minds and learning to walk in his will. We become disciples of the Holy Spirit and the body of Christ in order for this transformation to take place. Spending time alone with God allows us to enter into to the Holy of Holies, listening to his voice, praising his name and getting to know his Word. He is the only One that can fill our life with a joyous fascination enabling us to know who he is and who we are.

I believe this is a recurring theme in our lives with the Lord. It is apparent to me in my own life that as Rosanne, Rosanna Danna says, "There's always something." There is always something and it usually is due to my self-centered ways. Typically, my insecurity or pride causes problems because I take my eyes off Jesus and look at myself rather than him. It is only as I approach the throne of the King of all Creation accepting the fact that he always holds his scepter out to me exuberantly awaiting my arrival that I can let go of the pain, anger and resentments, which come through everyday life. It is there that we behold him and his glory and he changes us because we are unable to change ourselves. This enables us to walk in obedience to his Word.

"Rejoice evermore. Pray without ceasing. In everything give thanks; for this is the will of God in Christ Jesus concerning you." I Thessalonians 5:16-18

Rick Joyner stated this in a wonderful way in his book: Taking the Land, "We are called to live our present lives by the power and authority of the resurrected life of Christ. By its very definition, one cannot experience a resurrection without first experiencing a death. To be baptized with His baptism is to be conformed to the purpose of His death, the laying down of our own lives for the sake of others." **1**

Indeed, we are crucified with Christ; we walk together with other believers in the unity of the Spirit and the bond of love that can only come from God. This is a daily choice to live a life of humility and repentance depending solely on the grace of God to enable us in these areas.

We are living in a time where we will see the increase of God's kingdom expanding around us and in us. Lift up your eyes, look around you, and behold the glory of God over his people. Yes, there is darkness but His glorious resurrection power overcomes that darkness and draws people to the light that shines through you, dear saint of God. You are a new creation in Christ Jesus; walk in the newness of this life by serving the living God, Jesus Christ.

---

[1] Rick Joyner, *Taking the Land,* MorninngStar Publications 2008, **www.morningstarministries.org** pg. **148**

Journaling or Group Discussion Questions

1. What scriptures in this chapter had the greatest impact on you?

2. Journal about what God is saying to you through these scriptures.

3. What is God saying to you through Galatians 2:20?

CHAPTER 7

WE HAVE THE ARMOR OF GOD

"Finally, my brethren, be strong in the Lord, and in the power of his might. Put on the whole armour of God, that ye may be able to stand against the wiles of the devil. For we wrestle not against flesh and blood, but against principalities, against powers, against the rulers of the darkness of this world, against spiritual wickedness in high places. Wherefore take unto you the whole armour of God, that ye may be able to withstand in the evil day, and having done all, to stand. Stand therefore, having your loins girt about with truth, and having on the breastplate of righteousness; And your feet shod with the preparation of the gospel of peace; Above all, taking the shield of faith, wherewith ye shall be able to quench all the fiery darts of the wicked. And take the helmet of salvation, and the sword of the Spirit, which is the word of God: Praying always with all prayer and supplication in the Spirit, and watching thereunto with all perseverance and supplication for all saints; And for me, that utterance may be given unto me, that I may open my mouth boldly, to make known the mystery of the gospel, For which I am an ambassador in bonds: that therein I may speak boldly, as I ought to speak." Ephesians 6:10-20

The Helmet of Salvation

Isaiah 52 says Jesus' face was so brutally beaten and his entire body so disfigured that it was difficult to recognize him as a man. The blood of Jesus gushed from his face as Isaiah 53 depicts that he was marred beyond identification. There was nothing attractive or majestic about his appearance. The horrific, gruesome beating inflicted upon him serves as a reminder that this incomprehensible sacrifice is for us. Contemplate the excruciating pain he endured as his eyes were swollen shut, possibly gouged, his ears were shred, his mouth, teeth, chin and cheeks were bruised and bleeding beyond recognition. Then, He received a crown of thorns scorning his kingship.

Luke 22:64 says when they hit Jesus they asked him to prophesy, by telling them who hit him. This was not only an attack on his thoughts, attitudes, emotions and imagination, but it was a direct attack on the ministry of a Prophet. Sinful men rejected the testimony of the Creator of the Universe. Remember in Revelation it says, *"The testimony of Jesus is the spirit of prophecy."*

Consider also in Isaiah 53 that it was the Lord's good pleasure to make him an offering for our sin. He was acquainted with our deepest grief, rejection and hurt. Jesus our great High Priest offered his own blood for our sins.

This corresponds with the helmet of salvation, which protects our head from wounds. This includes thoughts, attitudes, emotions, imaginations and temptations. When we apply the blood of Jesus to these areas, we are able to reign victorious because of his suffering. Reflect on any temptation we may encounter, the Word of God proclaims there is no temptation for which God does not provide a way to escape. Ask Jesus to cover your eyes, ears and mouth with his blood and enable you to overcome temptation from the lust of the eyes, the things that you hear and your vocabulary or speech. Read the Word of God and plead the blood of Jesus over your thoughts and imaginations. Revelation declares that they overcame by the blood of the Lamb and the Word of their testimony and loved not their lives unto death. Take a moment to meditate on the penalty paid to purchase the helmet of salvation before we discuss the rest of the armor.

The Breastplate of Righteousness and Girding Your Loins with the Truth

Matthew 27 depicts that the soldiers scourged Jesus prior to delivering him to crucifixion. This signifies affliction greater than we can possibly imagine as the flesh literally frayed from his bones. The blood must have spurt from and covered his entire body. Isaiah 53 signifies he was whipped and beaten so we could be healed and whole. It coincides with the provision made by the breastplate of righteousness and having loins girt with the truth. These pieces of armor not only protect the body from injury, but also guard the heart from wounds. It indicates absolute wholeness.

Truth came by Jesus Christ and Ephesians 6 discusses having your loins girt with the truth. Loins can be indicative of the birthing place and the things we think about eventually give birth to our actions. Recently, I read Isaiah 53 says Jesus died without any descendents because he gave his life as a substitute for ours providing a royal inheritance. Our Father is the King of all creation. I believe that this not only provides for salvation and protection over our loved ones but also authority for the believer to come against curses and wiles of the devil. Our fight is not against flesh and blood, but against demonic strongholds.

Personally, at this time in history I believe many in the church do not have their loins girt with the truth. This truth buckled firmly around our waist will hold the breastplate of righteousness in place however if it is not we are open to the lies of the enemy. The lines are being drawn in the church over choices of righteousness and obvious sin but people are unable to see this because the belt of truth is not properly buckled around their waist leaving them open for unrighteousness to enter the heart. Much of America is now calling good evil and evil good making prayer for repentance and transformation a dire need. We expect this from the world because they do not have the armor of God in their arsenal of weapons, which means they do not know the truth.

As Christians, we maintain the Word of God is the truth, the standard by which we live our lives and it does not matter what the world thinks about it. We are also mindful that it is only by the grace of God that we stand and apart from it we can fall, this enables us to have compassion on people when they fall.

The Shield of Faith

Jesus sweat great drops of blood in the garden due to the depth of agony he was about to encounter and he petitioned the Father to let this sacrifice pass from him. If you ever wonder about God the Father saying no to any of his children, this may provide an answer to that question.

Reflect on your children and let me ask you if you have ever told them "no". Please take into consideration that even though you said "no" they had a choice to walk in compliance to you or rebel against your authority. What was the outcome? Jesus had the ability to choose whether to walk in submission or rebellion to the Father and his choice was obedience. We are likewise encouraged to run the race and rely on Jesus who authors and enables us to complete our faith, as stated in Hebrews 12. Jesus endured the cross because he had a vision of us and rejoiced in what he saw. These fiery darts advancing toward him in the garden caused him to sweat great drops of blood in agony but still respond affirmatively to the Father. We likewise can approach God with the fiery darts of the enemy assailing us and use the shield of faith Jesus provided through the shedding of his blood. Jesus agreed to a washing in his own blood to pay for our sins. How do we respond to him when he wants to wash us with the blood of Jesus? Again, consider a young child at bath time, do they respond affirmatively and say, "Awesome I cannot wait?" Most children do not, particularly if they are playing. Do we ever respond to the Lord negatively when he requests our cooperation with him in washing some aspect of dirt from our lives? Maybe I am not as sanctified as you are but I have been resistant, at times. The shield of Faith can seem weighty unless we remember that it is his shield and his strength, not ours. We are dependent upon his power.

"not by might, nor by power, but by my Spirit, saith the Lord of hosts." Zechariah 4:6

The Gospel of Peace

Jesus chose to be condemned to crucifixion as a criminal to bring to us the gospel of peace. He died for insurgents to demonstrate the incomprehensible love of God. The blood flowed from his hands and feet so we could stand on his word and proclaim the gospel to others. Wherever the Lord has us walking in life, we have the opportunity to carry the gospel of peace and to use our hands to serve, expressing his great love for the lost. We are to love those trapped in sin because we know what it is like to be there and can share the experience of freedom that comes only through Jesus. It is a marvelous honor to be ambassadors of heaven and servants to the King of All Creation.

"How beautiful upon the mountains are the feet of him that bringeth good tidings, that publisheth peace; that bringeth good tidings of good, that publisheth salvation; that saith unto Zion, Thy God reigneth!" Isaiah 52:7

The Sword of the Spirit

Isaiah 53 states Jesus' piercing for our transgressions acquired God's forgiveness for our rebellion.

When the soldiers pierced his side with the sword, both water and blood flowed out. 1 John 5:6 says God revealed Jesus Christ as his son by baptism in water and shedding of his blood. Remember the Holy Spirit descended upon Jesus at his baptism and the Father's voice thundered this is his beloved Son in whom he takes delight. The soldier's sword was to ensure Jesus' death, however the sword of the Spirit guarantees our life.

"For though we walk in the flesh, we do not war after the flesh: (For the weapons of our warfare are not carnal, but mighty through God to the pulling down of strong holds;) Casting down imaginations, and every high thing that exalteth itself against the knowledge of God, and bringing into captivity every thought to the obedience of Christ." 2 Corinthians 10:3-5

I do not know what your world is like but there are times when I can travel from zero to flesh in a nanosecond. One minute I am driving down the interstate worshipping Jesus with all of my heart and then someone cuts me off and I find myself saying, "watch where you are going, Jerk!" Suddenly, I feel the conviction of the Holy Spirit and begin to repent for speaking words that are worthless and not uplifting about someone that I may never meet. This is just one example of taking captive a thought, making it obedient to Christ through repentance, asking the Holy Spirit to take over and guard the door of my lips. Times like this are much easier to recognize than the subtle fiery darts that come at us to cause us to war against the kingdom of God. Yes, we war against the kingdom of God sometimes because the Kingdom of God is within us.

I never really considered myself at war with God's kingdom but the basic strategy of the enemy is to bombard us with thoughts actually aimed at God in others and us. These thoughts are fiery darts of the wicked one referred to in Ephesians 6. It usually begins with a subtle thought that we may easily cast down but as it continues to gnaw at us, questions may begin surface. The thoughts may seem to be about another person prompting us to ask, "Why did my husband, friend or child say that I am always late?" or "Why did I make that stupid comment to my mother?" or any variety of issues.

If I am struggling with a comment made by another person, I can go to them and ask them to clarify. Maybe, I am consistently late and I need to see this area of my life so that I can better plan my time.

The comment made to my mother may not have been stupid but the enemy might be attacking me because of an area in my life in need of healing. Did someone tell me that I was stupid as a child growing up, did it hurt my feelings causing me to draw back and live in self-protection mode? If I am hurt by a comment, I can embrace the pain and ask the Holy Spirit to fill me with the truth; then, I can forgive that person. It is critically important to acknowledge and embrace that pain in ourselves because when we live in denial of it, we cannot forgive because we claim there is no offense. When we acknowledge the pain, embrace it and then work through forgiveness, we launch an effective warfare over the enemy by using those divinely powerful weapons which breakthrough the strongholds.

"Confess your faults one to another, and pray one for another, that ye may be healed. The effectual fervent prayer of a righteous man availeth much". James 5:15

Confessing our sin is a weapon of warfare because it requires humility but also breaks the shame that can so easily entrap us when we try to hide our struggles. Remember the fig leafs in the garden as Adam and Eve tried to hide their nakedness from God. When we attempt to cover up our sins the fear of being exposed causes bondage because the enemy has us imprisoned in a lonely place. It is only as we become vulnerable that shroud of shame can be broken and we experience the freedom that comes through allowing others to bear our burdens. This openness with another brother or sister in the Lord actually demolishes the arguments and pretensions as we talk through them. There are times we need to talk things through and sometimes they are painful. I am by no means saying that this is an easy thing to do but it is a very powerful to take thoughts captive and bring them into the light where they can be destroyed.

The first strategic question the enemy used in the garden was, "Did God really say not to eat of the tree?" Immediately following the question, the host of fiery darts released designed to cast doubt on God's love and truth. The enemy has not changed and if we are mindful of the scriptures and the leading of the Holy Spirit in our lives, we can become more aware of these tactics aimed against us. I believe it is a continual process in life and as we experience various challenges, we have the constant opportunity for growth.

The goal of the fiery darts aimed at us is to prompt us to react on impulse rather than discerning the source. It is only as we discuss our feelings with God first and then a brother/sister in the Lord that we can gain insight into these strategic attacks. The key to winning the battle is relationship, which requires humility, repentance and love on our part. The enemy hates these things but his attacks can actually allow for transformation into our lives causing us to grow into the image of Christ. God's Word is the truth no matter what is happening in the world around us and that the enemy is a liar and the father of lies. Jesus Christ is the way, the truth and the Life.

Journaling or Group Discussion Questions

1. Can you identify an area of your life in which you find yourself continually struggling? (Journal about it)

2. Read over the scriptures in this chapter and ask God to speak to you about it.

3. What is God saying to you through James 5:15?

`

CHAPTER 8

YOU UNDERSTAND MY THOUGHTS FAR AWAY

"O Lord, thou hast searched me, and known me. Thou knowest my downsitting and mine uprising, thou understandest my thought afar off. ". Psalm 139:1-2

Reading Psalm 139 in his opening statement, the Psalmist, David, declares, *"You know everything about me, even when I am far away."*

There are times when I am far away and I find myself in anxiety and worry over situations in my life. Whether these situations health, provision, relationship or anything else, they are common to man. Do you realize God cares about your feelings when people are talking about you, when you are struggling to understand homework or do not know how you are going to meet your bills? God sees you when you are in your room alone crying over a situation in your life and I believe he weeps with you. You can sit down, discuss these insecurities with God and/or another Christian because they are common concerns, and have much to do with the power of God in us. I believe we underestimate God's understanding of our emotions, which distorts the truth of his Father's heart for us.

If you know Jesus Christ as your Lord, you have the Holy Spirit living inside you, the resurrection power of God longing to accomplish phenomenal missions. Many times, we equate these exceptional assignments only to the context of gifts of the Spirit or ministry but the power of the Holy Spirit has so much more for us. It is an extraordinary undertaking to live everyday life as a Christian because there are temptations and pitfalls all around us. Most of them are common everyday things like not participating in gossip, making a choice to humbly do what you dislike doing at work or maybe, saying no I cannot be part of this dishonest business practice knowing it may cost you a promotion or job. These may sound like simple everyday things but it takes the power of the Holy Spirit to make Godly choices. It is not about following the law but developing a relationship with God that will draw us to him for direction. It is a knowing just as David did that God is before me and follows me and he has placed his hand of blessing upon my head. This does not mean that God will necessarily answer us in the way we might expect however; as we commit the situation into his hands, we will receive the peace that passes understanding. King Saul was trying to kill David because he knew God called him to be the next king. David had several opportunities to kill Saul yet he chose not to because he would not touch God's anointed, even though he knew God ordained him. David patiently waited for God to open the door and fulfill that calling. How many times through the Psalms did David cry out to God for help or did he talk with his friend Jonathan (who also happened to be Saul's son)? What about Jonathan, who was best friends with David, knew the calling on David's life and was broken hearted over the sin of his father Saul? This must have been very difficult and I would venture to say that David and Jonathan spent time talking, weeping, and seeking God about how to handle the situation God's way. I believe Jonathan had to work through the feelings of hurt, anger and despair to come to the place of walking in forgiveness toward his father, Saul.

David and Jonathan are examples of developing friendships within the community of believers where we can share our struggles with and walk through life, bearing one another's burdens. This does not happen instantly because we must develop trusting relationships. Have you been hurt by friendships, people violating your trust, disappointing you or maybe even totally rejecting you? It is a fact that in this life, we will hurt others and others will hurt us. I am not sharing this to scare you or prompt you to hide in a corner somewhere to protect yourself because that is not what God has called us to do. In fact, getting us all alone where we cannot receive or reach out for support is a strategy of the enemy. So, how do we develop friendships and learn to trust again once we have been hurt? First is to talk with God honestly pouring out your heart to him Psalm 62:8). Read some of the Psalms and notice they are like journals about the Psalmist's feelings regarding a difficult situation. It usually begins with some intense feelings of what they would like God to do with their enemies as the Psalmist pours out his heart to God; then, as the Psalm ends there is usually somewhat of a resolve or answer. The next step, as God begins to bring relationship into your life is to allow it develop; and if it is difficult to trust so begin by sharing something small and build as you become more confident. Trust is not something we freely give, but people earn your trust as you develop the relationship.

It seems as we encounter trials and walk together through them it strengthens relationships. I am currently walking through some intense trials in my life and am so grateful that God is pouring his love upon me through his wonderful people.

Journaling or Group Discussion Questions

1. What kind of comfort do you find in the realization that Jesus knows everything about you and loves you tremendously?

2. Ask God to speak to you about how much he loves you.

3. What is God saying to you through Psalm 139:1-2?

CHAPTER 9

THROWING ROCKS

In the story of David and Goliath, David approaches Saul and says....

"And David said to Saul, Let no man's heart fail because of him; thy servant will go and fight with this Philistine. And Saul said to David, Thou art not able to go against this Philistine to fight with him: for thou art but a youth, and he a man of war from his youth." 1 Samuel 17:32-33

After discussion between David and Saul, Saul finally consents and permits David to fight. David approaches Goliath who is speaking contemptuously toward him, *"David replied to the Philistine, "You come to me with sword, spear, and javelin, but I come to you in the name of the LORD of Heaven's Armies—the God of the armies of Israel, whom you have defied. Today the LORD will conquer you, and I will kill you and cut off your head. And then I will give the dead bodies of your men to the birds and wild animals, and the whole world will know that there is a God in Israel! And everyone assembled here will know that the LORD rescues his people, but not with sword and spear. This is the LORD's battle, and he will give you to us!" 1Samuel 17:45-47*

"Reaching into his shepherd's bag and taking out a stone, he hurled it with his sling and hit the Philistine in the forehead. The stone sank in, and Goliath stumbled and fell face down on the ground." 1 Samuel 17:49

David was a young man, not a seasoned or popular warrior yet he obeyed the Lord and said, "I will." His obedient submission enabled the entire army of Israel to defeat the Philistine army. God gave David the boldness to approach the king and convince him to fight the giant.

David did not look to his abilities, his youth, and his status in life as a shepherd or his inabilities but to God who was the strength of his life. He allowed God to place him in an impossible situation because he had given his life to wholeheartedly love and obey God. This is just one example of how our impossibilities are God's victories when we walk in obedience to him. This became apparent in his response to Goliath: "You come to me with sword, spear, and javelin, but I come to you in the name of the LORD of Heaven's Armies—the God of the armies of Israel, whom you have defied."

It is amazing that David was able to kill Goliath with one stone and even more amazing that the stone sunk deeply into his head. The stone reminds me of the stone at the tomb of the resurrection because when rolled away from the grave it demolished the power of death. Jesus is the cornerstone and we are living stones fit together to bring glory to God. One important fact that we do not often consider when reading the story of David and Goliath is that though David killed Goliath, it took the army of Israel to defeat the Philistines. Obedience to God can greatly influence how we walk together as the body of Christ into victory. We all play a critical part in God's plan for His church.

A head is often symbolic of authority, such as the head of a company or the head of the Church is Jesus Christ. The fact that the stone sunk deeply into Goliath's head is symbolic his authority removed.

Goliath fell on his face after the stone hit him in the head. I often wondered why he would fall forward and not backward when hit from the front because it seems defy natural force. Again, as I pondered this I considered that falling on ones face before authority particularly God's authority is an expression of submission. Goliath did not willingly fall on his face but in the end, whether willingly or not all creation will bow to Jesus.

"And hath put all things under his feet, and gave him to be the head over all things to the church, Which is his body, the fullness of him that filleth all in all." Ephesians 1:22-23

"And the four and twenty elders and the four beasts fell down and worshipped God that sat on the throne, saying, Amen; Alleluia" Revelation 19: 4

This is certainly an example for us that even those that defy the Lord of Heaven's Armies will bow in submission to him one day. As living stones in his temple, the Lord lives in us so the cry in our hearts is to live in humble submission to him. This is a process that we must cultivate in our lives, affection based obedience to God is precious in his sight. David was a man after God's heart because he continued to pursue with a repentant heart of love toward him even after he sinned.

It does not matter if we are young, old, rich, poor, a world class leader or an everyday person God's love for us and his presence in us will accomplish more than we can possibly comprehend as we walk in obedience to him.

Journaling or Group Discussion Questions

1. What kind of things do you see as impossible in your life?

2. Talk to God about your feelings in these situations.

3. What is God saying to you as you meditate on the life of David?

CHAPTER 10

GOD'S MOST VALUED POSSESSION

"O Lord, thou hast searched me, and known me. Thou knowest my downsitting and mine uprising, thou understandest my thought afar off. Thou compassest my path and my lying down, and art acquainted with all my ways. For there is not a word in my tongue, but, lo, O LORD, thou knowest it altogether. Thou hast beset me behind and before, and laid thine hand upon me. Such knowledge is too wonderful for me; it is high, I cannot attain unto it". Psalm 139:1-6

What kind of God is so intimately acquainted with us that he leads us in the right direction even while we are yet unaware of circumstances arising in our midst?

It is beyond my comprehension to understand God's great love and even a small revelation of it brings a sense of awe and reverence that the God of all creation meets us where we are to bless us on our journey. Furthermore, I find an even greater astonishment that my responses are not always in accordance with my heart values so I find myself grieving and repenting for doing "those things that I do not want to do."

We cannot escape from him because everywhere we go he is already there; he created all things and planned for our arrival. He is there delighting in us and enjoys being with us so much that he rushes ahead to greet us and navigate us through each situation if we allow him to. He even saw us before we were born and had a plan previously set in motion for our good. Further expounding on this fact is:

"For thou hast possessed my reins: thou hast covered me in my mother's womb. I will praise thee; for I am fearfully and wonderfully made: marvellous are thy works; and that my soul knoweth right well. My substance was not hid from thee, when I was made in secret, and curiously wrought in the lowest parts of the earth." Psalm 139:13-15

He set our DNA in motion and stands back watching the beauty of his creation while it is forming.

Think of something you made that you are very proud of, or if you have children, consider the delight and joy they bring to your heart. Recently, as I was looking at pictures of my children when they were toddlers I came to the realization that they were the cutest kids I had ever seen, no I am not being biased, just stating the facts from the eyes of a mother. Now consider God watching us as we grow up in him and the thrill he experiences in his heart over us, his favorite children even while we were growing secretly in the womb. Next, consider the honor he has given us through medical science by allowing us to partake of this phenomenon using the miracle of the sonogram; we are not only able to see our children and discover their sex, but we can also see and hear their heartbeat.

"How precious also are thy thoughts unto me, O God! How great is the sum of them! If I should count them, they are more in number than the sand; when I awake, I am still with thee." Psalm 139:17-18

How is this even possible, I am one person and he has so many thoughts toward me that they would outnumber the grains of sand? The beach goes on for miles and miles, the desert can seem never ending, and as we drove by the Great Sand Dunes, it was windy that sand was everywhere. How many grains of sand are on the earth alone? How many are his thoughts towards his people on the entire earth? This idea is so immense that I ponder this thought, if God stopped thinking about me, would I cease to exist.

"Search me, O God, and know my heart; try me, and know my thoughts: And see if there be any wicked way in me, and lead me in the way of everlasting life" Psalm 139:23-24

God is preparing the hearts of his people for his great and ever-increasing presence.

God created us with specific needs and desires described in Psalm 139:1-6 is the need to develop relationship with him; he continually reveals his heart to us and desires intimacy with us. He knows everything about us; he rejoices and celebrates with us over things that no one else knows. He understands our hurts, misunderstandings, areas of shame and struggles with sin; even things we are unable to understand, articulate or even identify these areas in our lives.

He brings people into our lives to rejoice and weep with us as they comfort us with the same comfort they have received from God.

It is exciting that he knows our victories and our struggles with sin and he protects us by not disclosing the vast array of our sins and shameful deeds but instead honors us calling us kings and priests. He examines our hearts and knows all things. He even knows what we are going to say before we say it. I find that amazing because many times I do not know what I am going to say until it comes out of my mouth.

He encourages us to confess our sins one to another that we receive healing he has provided for us. When we do this, we are receiving the grace of God available to us through the other believers because we give and receive comfort from him. God is intimately acquainted with all of our ways and yet loves us in the midst of it. His great desire is for us to love him back with the love that he gave us through his Son Jesus Christ.

"Hear, O Israel; The Lord our God is one Lord: And thou shalt love the Lord thy God with all thy heart, and with all thy soul, and with all thy mind, and with all thy strength: this is the first commandment. And the second is like, namely this, Thou shalt love thy neighbour as thyself. There is none other commandment greater than these." Mark 12:29-31

"And hope maketh not ashamed; because the love of God is shed abroad in our hearts by the Holy Ghost which is given unto us." Romans 5:5

According to Romans 5:5 God empowers us to be passionate.

Mike Bickle from the International House of Prayer, Kansas City, once said at a "One Thing" Conference, "If you have nothing to die for, you will have nothing to live for. Many times when we struggle with depression it is rooted in a lack of passion and we are bored, unmotivated and tired because we were created to be passionate and wholehearted." **2**

These things can come from our own selfishness, woundedness or the enemy hitting us with negative thoughts because he is aware this truth. I am not saying this haphazardly or to bring condemnation because I struggled with depression and anxiety at various times in my life. The only way to get through these times is by continuing to press forward in relationship with the Lord and reach out to others even if we feel like isolating. Remember God is the only one that can lift us up out of the pit of depression and anxiety.

Shame and rejection often keep us in bondage while God's love drives the shame and rejection away as we make the choice to receive his love and pursue him with all of our hearts.

Frequently I sing a song over the body of Christ to let us hear his heartbeat and let us know his will. He is thrilled with us because we are his promised bride. Diamonds are given as a promise of marriage think of the beautiful stones placed in engagement rings and consider what a diamond looks like when it is held up to the light with its various facets of beauty. God made us that way and we can look at each other standing back beholding God's beauty, his glory as expressed through his creation. Think of the glorious array of colors reflected from diamonds as sunlight hits them, and then compare it to the beauty and glory that reflects from us as God's Spirit flows through us.

Mickey Evans has a wall at Dunklin Memorial Camp in Okeechobee with pictures of families that went through the drug program and its title reads, "Diamonds from the devil's junkyard." We are all diamonds in the hand of God.

We will stand in amazement as we consider the words in Psalm 139:5-6 that God walks before us and behind us; he is a shield about us protecting us as we go. He places his hand of blessing upon our heads each day and like the Psalmist, I find this knowledge too wonderful to comprehend.

David was a man known for possessing a heart after God; David found God captivating and he enjoyed spending time with him. Jeremiah also expressed his passion for God in the of Jeremiah chapter 15.

"Thy words were found, and I did eat them; and thy word was unto me the joy and rejoicing of mine heart: for I am called by thy name, O Lord God of hosts." Jeremiah 15:16

"One thing have I desired of the Lord, that will I seek after; that I may dwell in the house of the Lord all the days of my life, to behold the beauty of the Lord, and to enquire in his temple." Psalm 27:4

Enjoy each day, be blessed and take pleasure in the fact that the God who created you sees you as his most valued possession. You are special, a divine "let there be" and there is no one else, nor there ever anyone like you. You are a one-time design of the King of All Creation, so go forth in the joy and the love of our Lord Jesus Christ. We love him because he first loved us. God never forces us to love him but continually pursues us while giving us the choice to love him back.

---

[2] Mike Bickle, *One Thing Conference,* International House of Prayer, Kansas City, MO, http://mikebickle.org/resources/search/?search_terms=one+thing&x=22&y=14

Journaling or Group Discussion Questions

1. Take the time to prayer read Psalm 139 and enjoy the love of God washing over you.

2. What is God saying to you through Psalm 139?

2. Journal about what it means in your life to be God's most valued possession.

CHAPTER 11

CONTINUAL WONDER

Have you ever been awed or fascinated by God's creation; a new born baby, the majestic mountains, the beauty of a flower, butterfly, a sunset or the space shuttle going up? Sometimes we take these things for granted and do not stop to think how God has privileged us by allowing us to see babies in the womb or space shuttles going up into space, or some of the other marvels God allows us to behold. If you are a student, do you get excited about what you are studying; do you realize God created everything?

Have you ever wondered why you are living in this time-period, this country, in your particular family, surrounding issues and why God saved you? I realize this may be a strange question to many people but I have thought about this many times throughout the years. When I consider this, I begin to appreciate that God chose me specifically, for such a time as this. He selected each one of us and strategically placed us in the optimal position to fulfill his vision, write his story and complete his plans.

"But ye are a chosen generation, a royal priesthood, an holy nation, a peculiar people; that ye should shew forth the praises of him who hath called you out of darkness into his marvelous light; which in time past were not a people, but are now the people of God: which had not obtained mercy, but now have obtained mercy." 1 Peter 2:9-10

"Ye have not chosen me, but I have chosen you, and ordained you, that ye should go and bring forth fruit, and that your fruit should remain: that whatsoever ye shall ask of the Father in my name, he may give it you. These things I command you, that ye love one another." John 15:16-17

"...and who knoweth whether thou are come to the kingdom for such a time as this?" Esther 4:14

Okay, so you probably get the basic plan, love the Lord with all my heart, soul, mind and strength and love my neighbor as myself. I love the mandate to build relationship and bear fruit that will last to glorify God, loving God is the first and greatest commandment. You may be asking, "What is God's plan to establish this here in American right now in the body of Christ and how do you fit into it?"

"Let love be your highest goal..." 1 Corinthians 14:1 NLT

I listened to one of our pastors' speak about various issues facing the church and one in particular stood out to me as possibly one of the greatest challenges facing the American church today. We are a people that are so well educated that it is difficult to move out of rationalization and tradition into an experiential relationship with God. I am not talking about "warm fuzzies" but a relationship that brings us into communication and movement with his Spirit flowing through us. Please do not get me wrong, I love and encourage education, goal setting, tradition and common sense planning. It seems at times the above principles overshadow the freedom to move with his Spirit.

"Behold, I give unto you power to tread on serpents and scorpions, and over all the power of the

enemy: and nothing shall by any means hurt you." Luke 10"19

"It is the spirit that quickeneth; the flesh profit nothing: the words that I speak unto you, they are spirit, and they are life." John 6:63

"Finally, my brethren, be strong in the Lord, and in the power of his might." Ephesians 6:10

Think about being American and how treading upon demons and scorpions can sound ridiculous unless you are watching "Lord of the Rings" or some other movie. As for, the Lord's power, many would say, "I am a self-made man, I built this, obtained this, I did it myself."

In the book, Dressed to Kill by Rick Renner he discusses being strong in the Lord and in the power of his might. Below are a few sentences that really enlightened my view of the resurrection power available to every believer today.

"The word "power" is taken from the Greek word "kratos" (kra-tos), and it describes what I have come to call "demonstrated power."

The very same, exact identical kind of power that God used when he raised Jesus Christ from the dead, it is the very same, exact, identical power that is now at work in us ---*we have resurrection power!*

Because the word *kratos* is normally used to denote a demonstrated or outwardly manifested kind of power, this tells us that when this power begins to operate in us, it immediately seeks an avenue of release so that it might *demonstrate* itself.

In other words, this power doesn't come to us in order to sit idly by and do nothing. This power comes to accomplish some kind of *superhuman task." ~ from the book: by* Rick Renner, *Dressed to Kill* (Tulsa, OK: Teach All Nations, (1992) pp. 107, 109. **3**

Amazing, consider this mighty power of the Lord residing in you and begin to ask him what the superhuman task is that he wants to accomplish through you personally. Some people have a calling to minister in missions, schools, marketplace, as well as in the church.

"For the Kingdom of God is not in word, but in power." 1 Corinthians 4:20

"And what is the exceeding greatness of his power to us-ward who believe, according to the working of his mighty power, which he wrought in Christ, when he raised him from the dead, and set him at his own right hand in the heavenly places." Ephesians 1:19-20

"This is the word of the LORD unto Zerubbabel, saying, Not by might, nor by power, but by my spirit, saith the LORD of hosts." Zechariah 4:6

---

[3] Rick Renner, *Dressed To Kill* (Tulsa, OK: Teach All Nations, (1992), pp. 107,109.

The possibilities are endless and I will discuss this later but I want to get back to the American church. Now consider this mighty "kratos" power at work in us as we gather together with other believers. What could possibly happen when Christians gather in unity to worship and seek God? I sincerely pray there is expectation building up inside of you.

Consider God may want to bring healing and dealing of issues within the body of Christ as we are going out to the world or those less fortunate. Can you say, "It is me standing in the need of prayer?" This is transformation, not to be conformed to the patterns of this world but be transformed by renewing your mind.

"Now ye are the body of Christ, and members in particular. And God hath set some in the church, first apostles, secondarily prophets, thirdly teachers, after that miracles, then gifts of healings, helps, governments, diversities of tongues." 1 Corinthians 12:27-28

"O God, thou art terrible out of thy holy places: the God of Israel is he that giveth strength and power to his people. Blessed be God." Psalm 68:35

"Now there are diversities of gifts, but the same Spirit. And there are differences of administrations, but the same Lord. And there are diversities of operations, but it is the same God which worketh all in all. But the manifestation of the Spirit is given to every man to profit withal. For to one is given by the Spirit the word of wisdom; to another the word of knowledge by the same Spirit; To another faith by the same Spirit; to another the gifts of healing by the same Spirit; To another the working of miracles; to another prophecy; to another discerning of spirits; to another divers kinds of tongues; to another the interpretation of tongues: But all these worketh that one and the selfsame Spirit, dividing to every man severally as he will." 1 Corinthians 12:4-11

"The Spirit of the Lord God is upon me; because the Lord hath anointed me to preach good tidings unto the meek; he hath sent me to bind up the brokenhearted, to proclaim liberty to the captives, and the opening of the prison to them that are bound; To proclaim the acceptable year of the Lord, and the day of vengeance of our God; to comfort all that mourn; To appoint unto them that mourn in Zion, to give unto them beauty for ashes, the oil of joy for mourning, the garment of praise for the spirit of heaviness; that they might be called trees of righteousness, the planting of the Lord, that he might be glorified. And they shall build the old wastes, they shall raise up the former desolations, and they shall repair the waste cities, the desolations of many generations." Isaiah 61:1-4

"Faith works by Love." Galatians 5:6

How could this possibly change the culture of many American churches today if we began to see ourselves as vessels of God's power and put our education aside for God to use as a tool, if he so desired? What would happen if we put aside the ideals that encourage people inside the church to hide their own issues and only quietly discuss them with a professional counselor or an ordained pastor, so no one else knows? While this appears to be righteous, it actually robs people of accountability, relationship and freedom available through a loving body of believers. Openness promotes humility, healing, accountability, relationships, honesty, unity, breaking strongholds of pride, selfishness, shame and encourages everyday people to move in the gifts of the Spirit. I am not in any way suggesting that we advertise all of our problems in front of the entire congregation but rather than hiding, we encourage people to obtain help within the body of Christ. It is okay to confess your sin one to another and receive healing. We are human, we do face struggles, and it is a lie from the enemy that says, "If people really knew they would reject you." It is only as we honestly share our struggles with other believers that we can receive the love through them. What could happen if churches in American began having trainings, forums, meetings, studies and/or support groups to discuss every day issues such as Godly business practices, relationship struggles, drugs, sex, gangs, and other real life problems? It might prevent some from devastating falls, build strong support and allow people to comfort one another with the comfort that they themselves have received from God, building unity in the body.

When the church is in unity, we march off into victory conquering the enemy. There is a "kratos" (demonstrated superhuman power) within us, the Holy Spirit and he desires to release his power so we can walk in our calling. It begins with the humility of admitting that we are in the need of prayer, receiving that prayer and then going forth to testify.

I believe that we will see this happening in our churches and that the world will once again look at the church as a place to come for help. When I use the term church I mean, people are the church, we meet in a building. When we put the Gospel shoes on our feet, we will draw the world to Jesus Christ and instead of the church going to the world for help; the world will once again seek the church for help. Jesus said that if he were lifted up he would draw all men unto himself.

"But when the Comforter is come, whom I will send unto you from the Father, even the Spirit of truth, which proceedeth from the Father, he shall testify of me: And ye also shall bear witness, because ye have been with me from the beginning." John 15:26-27

"Howbeit when he, the Spirit of truth, is come, he will guide you into all truth: for he shall not speak of himself; but whosoever he shall hear, that shall he speak: and he will shew you things to come. He shall glorify me: for he shall receive of mine, and shall shew it unto you. All things that the Father hath are mine: therefore said I, that he shall take of mine, and shall shew it unto you." John 16:13-15

"Now when they saw the boldness of Peter and John, and perceived that they were unlearned and ignorant men, they marveled; and they took knowledge of them, that they had been with Jesus." Acts 4:13

"For the testimony of Jesus is the spirit of prophecy." Revelations 19:10

Yes, I believe the church is coming to a place where the manifestation of the Spirit will flow through us individually and corporately. God is at work in the hearts of people right now building deep relationship and preparing us for his coming revival. Many of our youth will stand as strong warriors against the kingdom of darkness. Some will be leaders in the marketplace, inventors, healers, missionaries, musicians, artists, etc. and will carry the power of God wherever they go. If you are a young person and sense God is planting something inside of you; go for it with all of your heart. Obey him, read the Word, pray and ask God questions. He says he will teach us all things and is the one that has knowledge of witty inventions. For example, if you want to be an engineer, designer, inventor, or whatever; study, pray get into the Word of God, ask him questions, journal and obey him. You are full of his resurrection power and it is an explosive power seeking an avenue of release through you.

" For wisdom is better than rubies; and all the things that may be desired are not to be compared to it. I wisdom dwell with prudence, and find out knowledge of witty inventions." Proverbs 8:11-12

"If ye love me, keep my commandments. And I will pray the Father, and he shall give you another Comforter, that he may abide with you forever; Even the Spirit of truth; whom the world cannot receive, because it seeth him not, neither knoweth him: but ye know him; for he dwelleth with you, and shall be in you. But the Comforter, which is the Holy Ghost, whom the Father will send in my name, he shall teach you all things, and bring all things to your remembrance, whatsoever I have said unto you. Peace I leave with you, my peace I give unto you: not as the world giveth, give I unto you. Let not your heart be troubled, neither let it be afraid." John 14:15-17, 26-27

If you are a banker, custodian, doctor, mother, secretary, adult, or father in the faith, God has a plan from the foundation of the world. Life is not over, it is just beginning because we have an eternity to live for him and serve him. It is amazing to me that scientist say we only use about 10% of our brains. When I hear that statement, I think yes here on earth but we have an eternity to grasp the wonders of God, which are beyond comprehension. I believe we will continue to learn and grow even after we leave this planet and join the great cloud of witnesses. God is bigger than anything we can possibly imagine and his plans for us exceed our wildest dreams.

God wants to demonstrate his power through us now and has some superhuman tasks to accomplish through us. We are his vessels and avenues of release. Go forth in victory mighty church of the Living God; you have resurrection power within you.

"For we are his workmanship, created in Christ Jesus unto good works, which God hath before ordained that we should walk in them." Ephesians 2:10

Begin to ask God to teach you everything and he will make it come alive to you. He says he will teach us all things and is the one that has knowledge of witty inventions. For example, if you want to be an engineer, designer, inventor, or whatever; study, pray, get into the Word of God, ask him questions, journal and obey him. Realize that you cannot accomplish anything without God and ask him to show you his remarkable secrets, pray "Lord, please teach me everything about your t-cell, or the speed of light or whatever it is you are studying." He will amaze you with his remarkable secrets as you spend time enjoying his company and conversing about his creation. He desires to do this because he says so in his word. He will fascinate you with his presence and the wonders of his creation. God, the creator of all things will impart his creativity to us if we ask him. When I was in seminary I took a class called, "Spirit-born Creativity" which taught me to seek God for creative ideas in writing, design, business, family, teaching and virtually every area of life. He has been faithful and is training me to walk in his Spirit and learn to be creative. He desires to do the same for you and waits for you to ask.

"Call unto me, and I will answer thee, and show thee great and mighty things , which thou knowest not." Jeremiah 33:3

"But the Comforter, which is the Holy Ghost, whom the Father will send in my name, he shall teach you all things, and bring all things to your remembrance, whatsoever I have said unto you." John 14:26

"I am the vine, ye are the branches: He that abideth in me, and I in him, the same bringeth forth much fruit: for without me ye can nothing ." John 15:5 & 7

God wants us to enjoy life and created things for us to enjoy, he breathed into man the breath of life and gave him authority over all his creation. He made man in his image, blessed him and placed him the garden to tend and enjoy. Stop for a minute and consider the fact that no two things that God creates are the same, not even twins. Every sunset, every flower, every snowflake and every human has a unique fingerprint of God on it; even our fingerprints (if we have them) are all different. Personally, I am unique because I have fingerprints that do not show up most of the time. Officials retake them until the machines can get a reading or I sign a waiver swearing that I am Deborah Neiberger. I am a unique individual created by God.

Journaling or Group Discussion Questions

1. What comes to mind when you think about God creating you for such a time as this?

2. Are there people in your life that you trust enough to talk with about hopes, dreams and struggles? Write or discuss your answer to the above question.

3. What is God what he is asking you to do today?

CHAPTER 12

CREATED TO ENJOY LIFE AND ENJOY GOD

He cares so much for man that when sin separated us from him he made provision to reconcile us back to himself through the death of his Son Jesus. When we accept this provision and invite Jesus to take over our lives there is an exchange made and the Spirit of God himself comes to take up residence in our heart. God's presence encompasses every part of our lives. There is no such thing as a secular and religious part of us because we are eternal beings. He is with us always, we cannot separate any part of our lives from him, and the Psalmist expresses this well in Psalm 139:7-12. We cannot escape him because he is wherever we may attempt to hide.

"Whither shall I go from thy spirit? or whither shall I flee from thy presence? If I ascend up into heaven, thou art there: if I make my bed in hell, behold, thou art there. If I take the wings of the morning, and dwell in the uttermost parts of the sea; Even there shall thy hand lead me, and thy right hand shall hold me. If I say, Surely the darkness shall cover me; even the night shall be light about me. Yea, the darkness hideth not from thee; but the night shineth as the day: the darkness and the light are both alike to thee. Psalm 139:7-12

God loves us and desires to spend time with us and he is excited to show us his love and manifest his presence to us and through us. Take some time to enjoy his presence when you are alone with him and in gatherings with members of the body of Christ. Begin to think about church as more than a place to -sit through a service but come expecting God's presence. Enter into the presence of God; cross the threshold of his gates with thanksgiving and his courts with praise realizing he loves spending this time with us. Psalm 22:3 says, "But thou art holy, O thou that inhabitest the praises of Israel." Consider that the Lord inhabits the praises of his people; he descends upon us, indwells and surrounds us. It is important to spend time in worship corporately and individually remembering that praise binds kings and kingdoms and nobles with fetters of iron (See Psalm 149). When we enter into praise, it drives the enemy away and he hates it because he tried to steal the praises from the Lord. It is very powerful to praise the Lord before entering into intercession because it opens up the heavenly realms, breaking down strongholds, preparing our hearts for Divine visitation because we are sharing our heart with the Lord and receiving his heart. When entering a church service pause to consider this celebration with the body of Christ and enter into the Holy of Holies. The Spirit and the bride say, "Come". Every part of the service has meaning and power beyond our ability to comprehend and as we receive minute revelations of it along the way, it astounds us. Take a few minutes; reflect upon various aspects of the church service, taking into consideration that the diamond with its many facets, it applies here as well.

The Communion Table - Jesus stated that as often as we partake of the bread and drink of the wine we are proclaiming his death and resurrection until he returns. We are making a proclamation to God, ourselves, the entire body of Christ, every person alive, and every created thing in heaven, earth and under the earth that we belong to Jesus. It is a powerful decree and indicative of giving ourselves fully and freely to Jesus. This proclamation shouts, "It is finished and into your hands, I am committing my spirit", we are agreeing with and embracing the cross in our lives and in our hearts. We are declaring that we are the bride of Christ and are consummating our marriage vows to the Lord Jesus Christ. The

Father has such a great love for us that he gave his only begotten Son so we will not perish, we are partakers of his suffering and in this covenant relationship, Jesus gave himself wholly for us and to us. God knows us completely, he knows every part of our hearts and he loves us. When we embrace the cross, we walk in the power of his resurrection, which is greater than anything we could possibly imagine. It takes time to assimilate this into our hearts, but as I meditate on this and the scripture, Romans 5:5, I can experience God's profound love and freedom.

I homeschooled my children for a few years when they were in elementary school and often included making dinner in my lesson plans to teach them to measure, set the table and plan a meal. In one of my lesson plans, I included a candlelight dinner to educate them about celebrating special occasions, as we often did for the holidays and their birthdays. This time they were going to help plan it from beginning to end and this dinner was to celebrate Dad's arrival home from work. The children were so excited and had so much fun that they wanted this to be a nightly event.

As I consider this, the revelation came that each week when we attend the Communion service we have a special banquet with Jesus. Many people work hard to organize this celebration with Jesus and it embarrasses me to think of the multitude of times I made light of it. The Holy Spirit brought conviction and taught me not to trivialize his great thanksgiving feast. As I contemplate this, I think of the words I read in The Hidden Power of the Blood of Jesus by Mahesh Chavda.

"There is no higher honor in the land than to eat at the king's table." **4**

We have this honor every time we partake of the Eucharist. Be blessed as you partake of the Lord's Supper Today!

" For I have received of the Lord that which also I delivered unto you, that the Lord Jesus the same night in which he was betrayed took bread: And when he had given thanks, he brake it, and said, Take, eat: this is my body, which is broken for you: this do in remembrance of me. After the same manner also he took the cup, when he had supped, saying, this cup is the new testament in my blood: this do ye, as oft as ye drink it, in remembrance of me. For as often as ye eat this bread, and drink this cup, ye do shew the Lord's death till he come." 1 Corinthians 11:23-26

These are profound prophetic words are words spoken from the lips of Jesus Christ with great thanksgiving to God that his death was part of the plan of salvation. I do not believe it is possible to grasp the depth of these words of love spoken to God and to us. Every time we partake of the Lord's Supper, we are honoring him, experiencing his presence, reaffirming our faith and proclaiming who he is to every living being. It is a great honor to partake of this love covenant at the communion table so rejoice in this as you go forth this day. God desires us so much that he gave his only son for us because he created us to reflect his beauty! We are so complex and our bodies are so intricate. It is fascinating to realize the detail God put into us and each one of us is different.

"For thou hast possessed my reins: thou has covered me in my mother's womb. I will praise thee; for I am fearfully and wonderfully made: marvelous are thy works; and that my soul knoweth right well. My

---

4 Mashesh Chavda, *The Hidden Power of the Blood of Jesus* (Charlotte, NC: Chavda Ministries International, (2002), pp. 111, 112. http://www.chavdaministries.org/

substance was not hid from thee, when I was made in secret, and curiously wrought in the lowest parts of the earth". Psalm 139:13-15

God placed inside of each one of us a legitimate craving to see his beauty in us. "And let the beauty of the LORD our God be upon us: and establish thou the work of our hands upon us; yea, the work of our hands establish thou it." Psalm 90:17

Some translations say beauty, some say favor, some say show us his approval, but the reality is he created each one of us with a unique expression of his glory. Just think about this truth if you have invited Jesus Christ into your heart the very Spirit of the living God resides in you.

God fashioned us according to his desire. We may not be satisfied with our physical appearance, intelligence or capabilities, but God is delighted. Our beauty attracts him. We may look at our imperfections and wonder, "How can I possibly be priceless to God?" God knows us completely and loves us so much that he sacrificed his son for us. He says that he has confidence in us and we are not deficient in anything.

Have you ever observed a child that carries a raggedy, old toy or blanket wherever they go? They cherish that toy as an article of value.

My daughter received a doll as a gift when she was a baby, named this doll "Mouth" and carried it everywhere she went. She loved Mouth even when Mouth was getting old and dirty. Valery enjoyed her new toys, but she still held Mouth in highest value, if Mouth was misplaced, Valery's heart was broken and we would search until we found her. When we found Mouth, she was excited, overjoyed to have her baby again. She did not treasure the extravagant or expensive toys she treasured Mouth.

God also sees us as his treasured possession because he is not seeking performance-based relationships, but cherishes us the way we are.

People spend thousands of dollars to become beautiful with everything from plastic surgery to make up and this is a legitimate yearning placed inside of us by God. It is not wrong to desire to look our best but if we determine our value by our appearances, we are missing the real beauty God has for us. I share this with hopes that you realize putting on makeup, having your hair fixed; getting a suntan, purchasing new clothes or doing other things to look good is not sin but rather the filling a yearning placed there by God himself. Can we go overboard in trying to fill this longing in the physical realm and miss the beauty that God placed inside of each person? Absolutely, God sees us as beautiful with or without the makeup and he wants us to realize that he sees us as favored and lovely whether we believe it or not, we are created in his image. Psalm 139 says God wove us together in our mother's womb, which appears to refer to speaking his "let there be" into our DNA strands commanding them to take shape in accordance to in his divine specifications. We are not the result of a sperm and an egg haphazardly crashing into each other as they journey through a woman's body; the King of all Creation spoke us into existence. God gave us a mind, a free will, emotions and physical strengths and weaknesses as valuable individuals with purpose and meaning. In the beginning, God had a plan and purpose for each one of us that spoke us into existence. Then, he carefully watched over us as we were growing inside of our mother's womb even before she realized we were there.

He cares so much for men that when our sin separated us from him he made provision to reconcile us back to himself through the death of his Son Jesus. When we accept this provision and invite Jesus to take over our lives there is an exchange made and the Spirit of God himself comes to take up residence in our hearts.

Journaling or Group Discussion Questions

1. What comes to mind when you think about God expressing his glory through you?

2. Do you consider yourself highly favored by God and why or why not?

3. What is God saying to you right now?

CHAPTER 13

CROWN, OIL AND GARMENT

"Thine eyes did see my substance, yet being unperfect; and in thy book all my members were written, which in continuance were fashioned, when as yet there was none of them." Psalm 139:16

God has a plan and a purpose for our lives and we will make a difference in the lives of others. He has come to make his home inside of us empowering us to fulfill his plans. God placed a desire inside of us to help others, to bring joy into their lives, to go to make disciples of all nations, feed the hungry, and love our neighbors, care for the sick, the widows and orphans.

"The Spirit of the Lord GOD is upon me; because the LORD hath anointed me to preach good tidings unto the meek; he hath sent me to bind up the brokenhearted, to proclaim liberty to the captives, and the opening of the prison to them that are bound; To proclaim the acceptable year of the LORD, and the day of vengeance of our God; to comfort all that mourn; To appoint unto them that mourn in Zion, to give unto them beauty for ashes, the oil of joy for mourning, the garment of praise for the spirit of heaviness; that they might be called trees of righteousness, the planting of the LORD, that he might be glorified." Isaiah 61:1-3

What has the Lord anointed us to do?
1. Preach good news to the poor
2. Bind up the broken hearted
3. Proclaim liberty for the captives
4. Opening of the prison to them that are bound
5. Proclaim the year of the Lord's favor
6. Proclaim the day of vengeance of our God
7. Comfort all who mourn
8. Provide for those who grieve in Zion
9. Bestow on them a crown of beauty, instead of ashes
10. Give the oil of joy, instead of mourning
11. Give the garment of praise instead of the spirit of heaviness

These are things God accomplished in Jesus and now wants to continue through us because the Spirit of the Lord is in us. God lifts us from the ashes, provides us with a crown of beauty, the oil of joy instead of mourning and places a garment of praise upon us removing the spirit of heaviness. Now that we have freely received of these marvelous gifts, we can freely give them to others.

Have you ever thought of yourself as a crown of glory in the hand of the Lord? The Lord holds us in his hands and he sees us as people of beauty expressing his glory for all to see. (Isaiah 62:3, Prov. 12:4) This is why he tells us to let our lights shine before men, so that they can see the good works done through us and give glory to God. (Matthew 5:16)

He gives us the oil of joy which is our strength (Nehemiah 8:10) and the beautiful garments of praise. A garment of praise reminds me of Joseph with his coat of many colors because praise is a colorful expression of our love for the Lord. Repeatedly throughout the Bible, we can read about these expressions of praise through singing, shouting, playing skillfully on instruments, expressions of praising God through our works.

The smallest acts of love and kindness express our praise to the Lord and have a powerful effect on the people around us. God allows little things in our lives to initiate changes that we cannot even begin to comprehend.

Sometimes the little things, the unexpected aspects of life can generate profound changes that display his amazing love for us. It is incredible to think that God records every day of our lives in his book and takes care of us and many times, we do not even notice. I share the story below as an example from my own life.

In the late 90's I was bit by a tiny tick in midst of beginning to build our business and ended up in bed with severe flu like symptoms. Expecting them to go away in a few days and return to life as usual, I took the week to rest. Instead, I became progressively weaker, suffered from severe chills, fever and profusely aching joints, which made daily life increasingly difficult. I honestly thought I was dying. Trying to keep up with daily life was nearly impossible and many days I could not even get up out of bed. There were times I sat in a hot tub seeking relief from numbness, blue fingers and chills. I was so cold that I could not sleep and thought it was abnormal considering I live in Florida.

During this time, my mother became ill with arrhythmia and I began driving to her apartment daily to be sure, she was okay and eating. Although she only lived a few miles away, I was so weak that I found it difficult to stay awake driving from back and forth. She decided to rent an apartment at an assisted living center because she wanted the security of the on-site nursing staff obviously seeing how sick I was.

Everyday life was challenging and owning a business made it even more demanding so after three years, I made a decision to close the business and work as a substitute teacher. This gave me the freedom to take jobs based on how I felt each morning and not concern myself with trying to make it through the week. Although I would miss speaking and training groups, I simply did not have the energy to pour into traveling, studying and building a business. It was a difficult decision but a wise choice considering our circumstances at the time. It also gave me the opportunity to work in the schools my children attended so I could spend more time with them.

After several years, through a multitude of antibiotics and herbal products, my health progressively improved and I am doing quite well today. I am so grateful to God for sparing my life and know it is because of his grace that I am alive today. There are mornings I wake up and look up at the beautiful moon and stars rejoicing in his incredible loving-kindness.

I am also learning to see God express his grace in many challenging areas of life.

Mom has been in a nursing home the last several years and the dementia causes her to travel back into earlier years of her life. There are a many times that she has not recognized me but mainly she thinks she is in a classroom, going out with friends, at work or somewhere else. I typically enter into her world because I realize I cannot make her live in the world around her. She asks about her parents, siblings, children, grandchildren and about people that I never met. I see this as God's grace because one day as we were talking, she suddenly said, "they all passed on right?" Then, she looked at me said, "It is really difficult to be here without the ability to do anything, having everyone take care of me, and if you did not come to see me I would have no reason to live". It was sobering to me and I realized that I would probably feel the same way. I appreciate now that living in the alternative world is one way God provides us strength to endure this difficult time of life. I also believe people in these situations encounter God in ways that we cannot begin to comprehend in life's daily routines. Mom continually talks about how good God is and how he has taken care of her over the years. She also speaks of things in her life that she would never talk about if she realized what she was saying. My emotions are mixed at times as I look at her and others in the nursing home, sometimes I cry when I leave but I am grateful to share in a little of her life.

"How precious also are thy thoughts unto me, O God! how great is the sum of them! If I should count them, they are more in number than the sand: when I awake, I am still with thee." Psalm 139:17-18

God yearns for us to spend time with him because he enjoys our company. He is not out to get us or squash us for doing wrong but looks at us with the love of a father. God's thoughts toward us outnumber the grains of sand and he desires the best for us.

How is this even possible, I am one person and he has that many thoughts toward me that they would outnumber the grains of sand? The beach goes on for miles and miles, the desert can seem never ending, and as we drove by the Great Sand Dunes, it was windy so we did not stop because the sand was blowing everywhere. How many grains of sand are on the earth alone? If his thoughts for just me outnumber the grains of sand, consider his thoughts of you, your family, the USA, the world, and it will overwhelm you. This idea is so immense it makes me wonder, "What if God stopped thinking about me, would I cease to exist?" This is not a doctrinal statement; simply a question from an enquiring mind wondering about the great and incomprehensible love of God. It will take an eternity to begin to fathom who he is and why he loves us so much. We are his dream house and he never leaves us because his precious Holy Spirit has taken up residence in our hearts. He claims full ownership and will continue to pursue us with his relentless love until we finally yield to him.

God thunders these words over you, "this is my beloved child in who I am delighted". Remember this whenever you hear the accusations coming from inside you. Speak forth this truth, "Jesus shed his blood for me and placed his treasured Holy Spirit inside me." Throw yourself on the mercy of the shed blood of Jesus and be reconciled to God.

"And so it is written, the first man Adam was made a living soul; the last Adam was made a quickening spirit. Howbeit that was not first which is spiritual, but that which is natural; and afterward that which is spiritual. The first man is of the earth, earthy; the second man is the Lord from heaven. As is the earthy, such are they also that are earthy: and as is the heavenly, such are they also that are heavenly. And as we have borne the image of the earthy, we shall also bear the image of the heavenly. Now this I say, brethren, that flesh and blood cannot inherit the kingdom of God; neither doth corruption inherit incorruption. Behold, I shew you a mystery; We shall not all sleep, but we shall all be changed, In a moment, in the twinkling of an eye, at the last trump: for the trumpet shall sound, and the dead shall be raised incorruptible,and we shall be changed. For this corruptible must put on incorruption, and this mortal must put on immortality. So when this corruptible shall have put on incorruption, and this mortal shall have put on immortality, then shall be brought to pass the saying that is written, Death is

swallowed up in victory. O death, where is thy sting? O grave, where is thy victory? The sting of deathis sin; and the strength of sin is the law. But thanks be to God, which giveth us the victory through our Lord Jesus Christ. Therefore, my beloved brethren, be ye stedfast, unmoveable, always abounding in the work of the Lord, forasmuch as ye know that your labour is not in vain in the Lord." 1 Corinthians 15:45-58 KJV

Jesus always brings us the victory. We stand on his promises because he paid our debit in full.

Journaling or Group Discussion Questions

1. Ask God what his thoughts toward you are at this moment.

2. Did you find the above question difficult to answer? What made the above question easy or difficult for you?

3. I encourage you to make time daily to read, meditate and journal about something you read in the scriptures daily.

BIBLIOGRAPHY

1. Rick Joyner, *Taking the Land,* MorninngStar Publications 2008, www.morningstarministries.org, pg. 148

2. Mike Bickle, *One Thing Conference,* International House of Prayer, Kansas City, MO, http://mikebickle.org/resources/search/?search_terms=one+thing&x=22&y=14

3. Rick Renner, *Dressed To Kill* (Tulsa, OK: Teach All Nations, (1992), pp. 107,109

4. Mashesh Chavda, *The Hidden Power of the Blood of Jesus* (Charlotte, NC: Chavda Ministries International, (2002), pp. 111, 112. http://www.chavdaministries.org/

www.ingramcontent.com/pod-product-compliance
Lightning Source LLC
Chambersburg PA
CBHW080526110426
42742CB00017B/3245